Revelation

INTERPRETATION
BIBLE STUDIES

Revelation

WILLIAM C. PENDER

WESTMINSTER
JOHN KNOX PRESS
LOUISVILLE · KENTUCKY

© 1999 William C. Pender
Leader's Guide © 1998 Westminster John Knox Press

Scripture quotations, from the New Revised Standard Version of the Bible are copyright © 1989 by the Division of Christian Education of the National Council of the Churches of Christ in the U.S.A. and are used by permission. All rights reserved.

The photographs on pages 1, 12, 25, 32, 42, 49, 58, 66, 80, and 95 are © 1998 PhotoDisc, Inc. All rights reserved. Used by permission..

Book design by Drew Stevens
Cover design by Pam Poll
Cover illustration by Robert Stratton

First edition
Published by Westminster John Knox Press
Louisville, Kentucky

PRINTED IN THE UNITED STATES OF AMERICA

09 10 11 12 - 10 9 8 7

Library of Congress Cataloging-in-Publication Data

A catalog record for this book is availablefrom the Library of Congress.
ISBN-13: 978-0-664-22858-3
ISBN-10: 0-664-22858-5

Contents

Series Introduction

The Bible has long been revered for its witness to God's presence and redeeming activity in the world; its message of creation and judgment, love and forgiveness, grace and hope; its memorable characters and stories; its challenges to human life; and its power to shape faith. For generations people have found in the Bible inspiration and instruction, and, for nearly as long, commentators and scholars have assisted students of the Bible. This series, Interpretation Bible Studies (IBS), continues that great heritage of scholarship with a fresh approach to biblical study.

Designed for ease and flexibility of use for either personal or group study, IBS helps readers not only to learn about the history and theology of the Bible, understand the sometimes difficult language of biblical passages, and marvel at the biblical accounts of God's activity in human life, but also to accept the challenge of the Bible's call to discipleship. IBS offers sound guidance for deepening one's knowledge of the Bible and for faithful Christian living in today's world.

IBS was developed out of three primary convictions. First, the Bible is the church's scripture and stands in a unique place of authority in Christian understanding. Second, good scholarship helps readers understand the truths of the Bible and sharpens their perception of God speaking through the Bible. Third, deep knowledge of the Bible bears fruit in one's ethical and spiritual life.

Each IBS volume has ten brief units of key passages from a book of the Bible. By moving through these units, readers capture the sweep of the whole biblical book. Each unit includes study helps, such as maps, photos, definitions of key terms, questions for reflection, and suggestions for resources for further study. In the back of each volume is a Leader's Guide that offers helpful suggestions on how to use IBS.

The Interpretation Bible Studies series grows out of the well-known Interpretation commentaries (John Knox Press), a series that helps preachers and teachers in their preparation. Although each IBS volume bears a deep kinship to its companion Interpretation commentary, IBS can stand alone. The reader need not be familiar with the Interpretation commentary to benefit from IBS. However, those who want to discover even more about the Bible will benefit by consulting Interpretation commentaries too.

Through the kind of encounter with the Bible encouraged by the Interpretation Bible Studies, the church will continue to discover God speaking afresh in the scriptures.

Introduction to Revelation

One of the verses to the old campfire spiritual "Do Lord" is "I read about it in the book of Revelation, you read it too," concluding with the chorus "Do Lord, oh do Lord, oh do remember me." For many of us, we have not "read about it in the book of Revelation." We have avoided a work that seems very alien to our faith and practice.

The bold task of this study, in line with the purpose of the entire Interpretation Bible Studies series, is to open up the book of Revelation in a way that makes it accessible and helpful to the church. The metaphor of opening up is apt, fitting the common title of this book of the Bible: "Revelation." This title comes from the opening words of the book: "The revelation of Jesus Christ" (Rev. 1:1). The underlying Greek word is *apocalypsis,* from which we derive the word "apocalypse" (another frequent title for this book is the Apocalypse of John).

Apocalypsis, or "revelation," means uncovering, disclosing, bringing into the light, opening up. The book's avowed purpose is laying out the revelation of Jesus Christ. One quirk in our common references to this book is to speak of the "book of Revelation*s,*" as if it were plural. It is not. It is the singular revelation of Jesus Christ.

Before we get lost in fantastic imagery and speculative applications to our times, the first "opening up" is that this book of the Bible is about revealing

"The vision of John"

Jesus Christ, and not about spelling out details of the end of the world or curiosities about heaven and hell. This book points to the presence of the risen Christ in the midst of a troubled and threatened community of faith.

One of the basic concerns of this study is to answer the question, "How was this book received in its first-century setting?" In other words, what was this book "revealing" to those who met for worship on the Lord's Day in Ephesus, Sardis, and other congregations in the Roman province of Asia? What will be revealed to us will not correspond directly to our time and place; the book was not written to us. It makes no sense to say that the book of Revelation reveals entities like the United States, Russia, or the modern state of Israel. However, even though the book is not addressed to us, we will find faithful words to prod and to comfort us in our life of faith.

Like other texts of scripture, the book of Revelation is a minority report. It does not even represent the entire spectrum of faith in the Roman province of Asia at the end of the first century. It is a limited expression of faith and needs to be balanced by the other sixty-five books of the canon. However, it is a part of scripture. It has a faithful word to the church. My hope is that, in these ten units, you the reader will find this to be so. If you do not find it to be so, it is the fault of this interpreter rather than Revelation itself.

The reflections that follow are my own, but I look at the book of Revelation through the eyes of others. Chief among these other "eyes" is the work of M. Eugene Boring, whose book in the Interpretation commentary series superbly lays out the broad context of the study of Revelation as well as addresses the purpose of individual passages. Another frequent friend in my mental and spiritual conversation with the book of Revelation is Eugene Peterson, who wrote the book *Reversed Thunder: The Revelation of John and the Praying Imagination.* Peterson has a wonderful eye and ear for the artistic and poetic function of the book. His perspective disarms many of the literalistic understandings of Revelation that make it so daunting for many readers. Finally, for digging into each verse and uncovering detail after detail, the work of Robert H. Mounce in his commentary *The Book of Revelation* has been very helpful. (See the bibliography for fuller details of each of these books.)

I claim the author's privilege of saying "thank you." Thank you to the teachers, ministers, and professors who taught me that the whole Bible is the Word of God, even the book of Revelation. Thank you to the session of Oakland Avenue Presbyterian Church in Rock Hill,

South Carolina, for allowing me to use continuing education time to write. Thank you to the Roots and Wings class of that congregation who have let me air the reflections that came together for this book. Thank you to Ann Wilkerson, who said quite sincerely that she enjoyed proofreading and marking up the rough drafts. Thank you to my wife, Sheri, and three children—Joshua, Amy, and Julia—for putting up with my time away and "writer's grouchiness."

Want to Know More?

About the book of Revelation? See M. Eugene Boring, *Revelation*, Interpretation (Louisville, Ky.: John Knox Press, 1989); William Barclay, *The Revelation of John*, 2 vols., rev. ed., Daily Study Bible (Philadelphia: Westminster Press, 1976); Charles H. Talbert, *The Apocalypse: A Reading of the Revelation of John* (Louisville, Ky.: Westminster John Knox Press, 1994); C. Freeman Sleeper, *The Victorious Christ: A Study of the Book of Revelation* (Louisville, Ky.: Westminster John Knox Press, 1996); and Catherine Gunsalus González and Justo L. González, *Revelation*, Westminster Bible Companion (Louisville, Ky.: Westminster John Knox Press, 1997).

"I read about it in the book of Revelation, you read it too." What I read about is Jesus Christ, who does not just remember the community of faith but stands with it. What I read about is the presence of the risen Christ to sustain us in this life and the life to come:

> Listen! I am standing at the door, knocking; if you hear my voice and open the door, I will come in to you and eat with you, and you with me. To the one who conquers I will give a place with me on my throne, just as I myself conquered and sat down with my Father on his throne. Let anyone who has an ear listen to what the Spirit is saying to the churches. (3:20–22)

May you read about it too in the book of Revelation.

1

The Call to Keep What Is Written

G. K. Chesterton said of Revelation that "though St. John the Evangelist saw many strange monsters in his vision, he saw no creature so wild as one of his own commentators" (Chesterton, 29). In joining the company of those commentators, at least one goal is not to join Chesterton's wild bunch, whose number are legion. Recent history might include David Koresh and the Branch Davidians in Waco, Texas, and Hal Lindsey, whose book *The Late Great Planet Earth* was the best-selling American book of nonfiction in the 1970s and who wrote subsequent, widely read books with titles such as *The Last and Future World* and *The Terminal Generation* (see Collins, 232).

For centuries, the book of Revelation has been the supposed source of much turmoil in the church—"supposed" because the turmoil is foisted upon the book rather than the book instigating the turmoil. For example, in the standoff between law enforcement negotiators and David Koresh, the leader of the Branch Davidians in Waco, Texas, one of the negotiating items was giving Koresh time to finish his interpretation of Revelation. However, it was not the encounter with the book of Revelation that drove David Koresh over the edge. His own tormented vision hooked into the book, twisting its meaning and intention. The church's greatest difficulty with the book of Revelation has been with those who have misused the text.

> "One of the many unhelpful myths that abound with regard to Revelation is that through the centuries everyone has arbitrarily interpreted the book in his or her own way, resulting in an endless variety of interpretations, a trackless jungle."—Boring, *Revelation*, Interpretation, 47.

As a result, the frequent strategy has been to give up on Revelation, either by conscious choice or by neglect. For example, the Common Lectionary includes only a few passages from Revelation. The historical precedent for this cursory use of Revelation reaches back to the Reformation and earlier. The reformers Martin Luther and Ulrich Zwingli basically gave up on the book of Revelation. John Calvin wrote a commentary on every other book of the New Testament, but conveniently left out Revelation. And, in fact, the objections to the use of Revelation go back to the earliest centuries of the church.

The task in this first unit and the succeeding units of this study is to see how we can benefit from the serious reading of Revelation as part of scripture, a part of that document which in a variety of ways is the Word of God to us. The task is to claim the blessing of Revelation: "Blessed is the one who reads aloud the words of the prophecy, and blessed are those who hear and who keep what is written in it; for the time is near" (1:3).

> "Blessed are those who hear and who keep what is written in it."—Revelation 1:3

Literary Genre

With the exception of the latter half of the book of Daniel, the book of Revelation is unique among the sixty-six books that make up our scripture. Because there is so little quite like it in our Bible, modern readers often fail to note that it is part of a large body of literature that was produced by Jews, Christians, Greeks, and Romans. This kind of work, this genre, is often called apocalyptic literature.

I can pull off my bookshelf a volume titled *The Old Testament Pseudepigrapha: Apocalyptic Literature and Testaments.* It contains 995 pages of small print, excluding the 36-page introduction (it makes a very nice bookend to hold up other books!). It is a collection of literary documents and fragments that were relatively contemporaneous with Revelation. Although often strange to our sensibilities and thoughts, the book of Revelation stands within a whole series of literary works that share many of the same "set pieces." These "set pieces" in apocalyptic literature include such things as conversations with angels, trips to heaven, judgment scenes, earthquakes, the sun turning black, fascination with numbers, and so forth.

In some ways, it is like the television commercial for a particular brand of spaghetti sauce, where the Italian mother is suspicious of the off-the-shelf spaghetti sauce. "What about the basil?" is the question the mother asks of the daughter. "It's in there," comes the response. "What about the garlic?" says the wary mother. "It's in there," repeats the daughter. "What about oregano?" a still-worried mother queries. "It's in there," says the daughter once again. When it comes to spaghetti sauce, implies the commercial, there are certain items that are expected be "in there."

"[A professor] used to tell his classes of a student who complained, 'I don't understand Revelation, but every time I read it, I feel like singing.' 'That is understanding it!' was the reply."—William R. Ramsay, *The Westminster Guide to the Books of the Bible* (Louisville, Ky.: Westminster John Knox Press, 1994), 513.

When it comes to apocalyptic literature, there are some things that one expects to see. For most modern readers, unfamiliar with the corpus of apocalyptic literature, the great and fantastic variety of Revelation strikes us as unique. But much that we find here is what was "expected" in this sort of literature. The fantastic visions are the means of expression.

Biblical Context

We need to see the book of Revelation in its literary context. We also need to see it in relation to the rest of our Bible. In some ways, it would be fair to say the book of Revelation says nothing that has not already been said in the previous sixty-five books of scripture. What is new in the book of Revelation is a new way to say it. What is new is not the content, but the means of saying it.

For example, in the 404 verses of the book of Revelation, there are more than 500 allusions to the Old Testament. These Old Testament references are allusions, because there are never any direct quotes, only phrases and images.

The book of Revelation is thus a montage, a mosaic, a collection of Old Testament phrases that pile on top of each other. For an audience of the first century, steeped in the Hebrew scriptures (and their Greek translations), these allusions would ring loudly. By and large, we are somewhat deaf to them and need hearing aids—or study aids—so that we can see how the allusions pile up on each other.

"The God who speaks here is not a different God from the one heard in the words of the biblical prophets."—Boring, *Revelation*, Interpretation, 64.

Consider this example. Suppose I wanted to make a movie about a woman named Scarlett. Scarlett, together with her dog Toto and her butler named Rhett, take in some children whose mother has died. Confronting the children's grief, she tells them that tomorrow, and each day after that, is another day. Scarlett builds up the children's faith so that they will be prepared to climb every mountain, to stay fixed on the few favorite things that make them happy. Somewhere—perhaps somewhere over the rainbow—Scarlett, her dog, and the butler will find happiness for these children, and there will be sounds of music.

Now, if you have seen *Gone with the Wind, The Wizard of Oz,* and *The Sound of Music,* you catch the rather obvious "borrowings" that are going on. If you haven't seen *Gone with the Wind,* then the name "Scarlett" and a butler named "Rhett" will mean no more than names taken at face value.

The book of Revelation is a montage of Old Testament allusions. It rings of the Old Testament. So, in some ways, it may be said that in compacting more than 500 Old Testament allusions in 404 verses, there is nothing new in the book of Revelation—only a new way to say it.

The Writer

We know his name is John; he tells us that. What he does not say is which John he is. John was as common a name in ancient times as it is today. He does not claim to be the apostle, the brother of James and the son of Zebedee; he gives no indication that he was a fisherman; he does not refer to particular aspects of Jesus' earthly ministry beyond the fact that he was crucified and was resurrected by God. He is just John.

Within the next hundred and fifty years after the book was written, there was debate in the church about whether this John was the apostle John, the son of Zebedee. Some said it was; others said no. Frankly, it may not matter. What we have is a work of a man who was banished from his home because of his Christian faith. He became a refugee, unable to return home, living on the island of Patmos in the Mediterranean Sea. We know that social ostracism, economic oppression, and the beginnings of state persecution for Christians were already at hand and threatened to get much worse.

We may not get very far in saying much about the biography of this man named John, but we can say what he does in his work. We can speak of his vocation or his calling, evident through the book of Revelation. And it is threefold: theologian, poet, and pastor (Peterson, 4–8).

John the Theologian

Revelation 1:2 declares that he, John, bears witness to the word (which in Greek is *logos*) of God (which in Greek is *theos*). From these two words, *theos* (God) and *logos* (word), we get our word theology: the word about God, "God-talk."

There are pressures to reduce God to only that which we cannot explain or understand, to only those experiences where we are up against the limits (as in the old saying that there are no atheists in foxholes). God is pushed out to the periphery of our experience; few can say with much conviction that we have experienced God.

> **Why was John sent to Patmos?**
>
> Boring (81) writes that Patmos was "a small island about seventy-five miles west of Ephesus. Archaeological evidence indicates that in John's time Patmos was a fortified island belonging to Miletus, with a quality Greek school and shrines to Artemis and Apollos. There is no evidence of its being a 'penal colony,' but the island was used by the Romans as a place of banishment for troublemakers, real and potential."

> The theologian offers his mind in the service of saying "God" in such a way that God is not reduced or packaged or banalized, but known and contemplated and adored, with the consequence that our lives are not cramped into what we can explain but exalted by what we worship. (Peterson, 4)

We need theologians who keep us thinking about God, not ignoring God or making random guesses. We need persons like John who bring together *logos* (word) and *theos* (God). We are, in some sense, human because of our capacity to create and use words. To bring words together with God is to render some sense to the chaos around us. Otherwise the world is a madhouse of ecological disasters like oil spills and holes in ozone, of nuclear disasters about to happen (we can destroy the world if we use the accumulated might in our arsenal), of personal disasters of illness, suicide, addiction, failure, meanness of spirit.

> "John's hope for the future is not based on some hidden discovery of exactly how or when the end will come, but on what was then, and is today, at the very heart of the Christian faith: that we need not fear the final outcome of history, for we have seen its face in Jesus Christ."—González and Gonázlez, *Revelation*, Westminster Bible Companion, 10.

We need theologians to say a word about God that cuts through the chaos and brings us life. And John is a theologian.

John the Poet

John is also a poet.

> A poet uses words not to explain something, and not to describe something, but to make something. Poet (*poétēs*) means "maker." Poetry is not the language of objective explanation but the language of imagination. We do not have more information after we read a poem, we have more experience. If the Revelation is written by a theologian who is also a poet, we must not read it as if it were an almanac in order to find when things are going to occur, or a chronicle of what has occurred. (Peterson, 5)

A poet is an artist who writes for us to see, smell, feel, touch, and hear a new reality or, at least, a new perspective on reality. The words elicit an experience that then can be thought through and analyzed, but first the artist and the poet seek to make us experience their reality.

Take, for example, the poetic line from Carl Sandburg about the fog coming in "on little cat feet." If we read that for knowledge, then we will be outside looking for paw prints in the dew. Instead the words are meant to create an experience of the subtle and quiet way that fog arises.

Artistry—the creation of experience—is part of the scripture, not just the book of Revelation. Consider the first book of the Bible, Genesis; it could have begun with the very straightforward statement that all human beings rebel against what they know is right. There is not a single one of us that does not stray. That is one way to say it.

But what if I begin, "There was a grand and large garden, watered by rivers, with the animals at peace with one another. And in the shade of the trees, man and woman walked hand in hand in harmony with the plants and animals and their God. All was there for them—all except the one tree from which they were not to eat . . . "

You know the story. Who can hear that story and not conjure up in their minds an image for sight, sound, smell, taste, and touch? The artistry of the story is for us to experience the fall of humanity from that state of peace with God and the world. Even if all we were supposed to do was to keep one commandment, still we would break it. That is, in part, what the story is about. The point is never said, but rather made through the experience of telling the story.

John, the theologian, is a poet, an artist, a maker of experience. His fantastic visions and words are meant to give us an alternative view of the world, one that glimpses the divine purpose in all things and events.

John the Pastor

John's passion for thinking and talking about God and his genius for subjecting us to the power of language so that the images are reborn in us, connecting us with a reality other and more than us, that is to say, his theology and his poetry—these are practiced in a particular context, the community of persons who live by faith in God. What he talks of and the way he talks of it take place among persons who dare to live by the great invisibles of grace, who accept forgiveness, who believe promises, who pray. These people daily and dangerously decide to live by faith and not by works, in hope and not in despair, by love and not by hate. And they are daily tempted to quit. (Peterson, 7–8)

John stands among such people as a pastor. As he puts it, "I, John, [am] "your brother who share with you in Jesus the persecution and the kingdom and the patient endurance" (1:9).

John is not our pastor; he was not writing to any of us. He stands in the middle of his people who lived by faith in the first century. People who live by faith are always "in the middle."

The beginning may be known: "God saw everything that he had made," declares Genesis 1:31, "and indeed, it was very good." The end may be sure: "Then I saw a new heaven and a new earth," declares John later in his book (21:1). A good beginning and good ending, but we stand in the middle where we are constantly caught off guard by the eruption of evil: debilitating disease, family violence, shootings in schools, tornados ripping through churches on Sunday morning, marriage breakups, abusive taxing authority.

"Christ appeared, not to dazzle but to communicate a message. John obediently writes."—Boring, *Revelation*, Interpretation, 85.

John's list of evil erupting in the middle of our lives would be longer: getting beat up like Rodney King but with no public outcry at the brutality; getting excluded from an opportunity for a job, with no option for filing a lawsuit; being run out of one's home like a Bosnian Muslim or a Kosovo Albanian, with no international outcry; and—in an extreme situation: getting nailed to a cross. Such are the potential consequences for carrying the name Christian. In the middle, despite a good beginning and a good ending, there are disappointments, contradictions, not-to-be-explained absurdities, and bewildering paradoxes.

A crucifix on the present-day island of Patmos.

> The pastor is the person who specializes in accompanying persons of faith "in the middle," facing the ugly details, the meaningless routines, the mocking wickedness, and all the time doggedly insisting that this unaccountably unlovable middle is connected to a splendid beginning and a glorious ending. (Peterson, 8)

John is a pastor: he is not interested in giving us the temperature of hell or describing the furniture of heaven. When we read Revelation as a pastoral expression, the interpreter can assume "that John had a message to the churches to which he was writing which concerned their own situation, that they understood the message, and that the modern interpreter cannot accept any interpretation of the book which its first readers would not have understood" (Boring, 50–51). John does not care about times and judgments and blessings in and of themselves. Every word, every number, every vision, every song, every symbol is meant for immediate use by his first-century readers, his pastoral charge. He was a pastor.

The book of Revelation has meaning upon meaning in its 22 chapters, its 404 verses. No interpreter ever gets at it all; no generation ever dries out the well of

Want to Know More?

About apocalyptic literature? See M. Eugene Boring, *Revelation*, Interpretation, 35–46; William Barclay, *At the Last Trumpet: Jesus Christ and the End of Time* (Louisville, Ky.: Westminster John Knox Press, 1998), 1–17, 85–93.

About the different types of literature in the Bible? See James L. Bailey and Lyle D. Vander Broek, *Literary Forms in the New Testament: A Handbook* (Louisville, Ky.: Westminster John Knox Press, 1992).

meaning in it. When we approach it as the church today, we listen recognizing its literary genre, its Old Testament base, and the situation of the author, John—whose subject was God, not esoteric details (he was a theologian); whose venture was imaginative and creative not dogmatic and literalistic (he was a poet); whose immediate concern was the first-century reader to whom he claims to be a brother, for he was in the middle with them (he was a pastor).

And this man named John wrote this book and declares: "Blessed is the one who reads aloud the word of the prophecy; and blessed are those who hear and who keep what is written in it; for the time is near" (1:3).

? Questions for Reflection

1. The book of Revelation has been characterized as strange and difficult to understand. If it is such a put-off, why study this book? Is the book of Revelation optimistic or pessimistic? Why so?

2. John begins and ends this book (compare 22:10) with the phrase "the time is near." To what do you suppose he is referring? Using a concordance, find other references in the Bible to time being "near." How do these other references illuminate your understanding of John's use here?

3. John's request is for his hearers (readers) to keep what is written. What do you think he means? What are things that you keep, either literally or figuratively? Why?

4. According to the writer of this study, Revelation contains some "set pieces" or "stock images." When one sees or hears these images, one expects a certain type of experience. Our task is to identify those images and connect them correctly to the right type of experience. What are some experiences that have "set pieces," that is, ones you expect to find certain characteristics associated with? What expectations do you bring when speaking about God or God's will?

2 Revelation 1:12–20

One in the Midst of the Lampstands

John the Seer writes to his pastoral charge because he has a vision of Christ. But his vision is not of Jesus of Nazareth walking along the Sea of Galilee, but of the risen, triumphant Lord who stands within and above history. As we consider this vision, we need to remember two features of John's expression: First, John's descriptive language rings of the Old Testament, in the main from the books Daniel, Exodus, Isaiah, and Ezekiel. John is weaving together descriptive language of the Old Testament. As noted in the previous chapter, John does not say anything new; he says it in a new way. It is a vision, but the content of the vision is set by the Old Testament.

As has often been said, in the first century Jesus was the unknown that needed definition. What was known was the Old Testament, the book of the people of God. One of the tasks of the early church was to explain this Jesus in terms of what was known, the Old Testament. So John's vision of Jesus is a montage, a mosaic, a gathering together of Old Testament references.

Second, John's descriptive language is symbolic and metaphorical, and is not meant to say this is how Jesus really looks. It is intended to have a cumulative effect on the hearer.

If you take the language of the vision literally, you have all sorts of problems. In other words, if we took this vision down to the police station and presented it to an artist who can draw a picture based on a witness's description, the artist would be hard pressed to render a drawing. For example, how can a person have a sword com-

> "The use of such language is an expression of his conviction that 'God' is to be defined as 'the one who has revealed himself definitively in Jesus.'"—Boring, *Revelation*, Interpretation, 83.

ing out of his mouth? If Jesus' face shone like the sun, which is blinding light, then how could John see the facial features of mouth, eyes, and hair? If Jesus holds seven stars in his right hand, how can he then place his right hand on John's shoulder? Taking the language literally can lead to absurdity.

Think of it this way: Four people attend a fireworks display; one says, "It was bad." The other says, "It was groovy." The third says, "It was magnetic gorgeous." The fourth says, "It was hip." If you take their comments literally, then you have that the fireworks display was poor, it had grooves in it, it tugged on iron and steel, and it was part of the anatomy.

Taken cumulatively and not literally, however, you come to the conclusion it was a well-done, well-executed fireworks display. The descriptive language of John's vision is meant to have that sort of cumulative effect. It is not meant to be put together in a literal picture.

The Vision of Christ

On the pulpit in the chapel at Columbia Theological Seminary (the Presbyterian seminary in Decatur, Georgia), there is a plaque mounted on the back of the pulpit where only the preacher can see it. The words, in large block letters, are a quotation from the Gospel of John about some Greeks, some non-Jews, who come seeking Jesus. And these Greeks say to Phillip, one of the disciples, "We would see Jesus" (John 12:21, RSV). Every preacher in the Columbia Seminary chapel is confronted with this quotation, this request, "We would see Jesus."

"We wish to see Jesus."—John 12:21

The Jesus that John sees is not the Jesus, meek and mild, not Jesus the Socratic teacher who asked penetrating questions, not the Jesus who was tired and weary after long walks, not the Jesus who welcomed little children in his arms. No, through the eyes of the visionary John, we see another Jesus: a Jesus meant for a troubled and fearful church, a Jesus meant for a church that is tempted to accommodate, to fit in without rocking the boat.

Like the artistry of impressionistic painters such as Vincent van Gogh, the description is not realistic but impressionistic. Most of us have seen reproductions of van Gogh's paintings, if not the actual paintings. His paintings are done in brilliant colors, but not with

15

photographic realism. Such is John's vision: it is in brilliant, impressionistic colors. John's vision has the shimmer of a brilliant rainbow.

The colors of John's rainbow vision of Jesus radiate primarily from the Old Testament. The colors on his palette come from Old Testament imagery. Unless one knows the Old Testament, one is in some sense color blind to the total effect. It is a rainbow effect of colors merging together. It must be experienced in its totality first, and then broken apart into component colors. What we do with the vision is see the whole, and then we can step away and unweave the rainbow.

The Lampstands

Jesus, the rainbow of Old Testament colors, is set in an unusual sky. John sees Jesus standing among seven golden lampstands. These are not individual candle holders, but rather golden stands, each holding a container of oil. We do not use golden lampstands today; we have electric lights. But golden lampstands were reserved for places of worship: for the high and holy times (similar to the way candles might be used in a Christmas Eve service). And we are specifically told a few verses later (Rev. 1:20) that these lampstands represent the seven churches to whom John is writing.

Where is Jesus found? Standing in the midst of the churches. We have this grand vision of Jesus Christ, and he stands among the churches. You would think Jesus could find a better place to stand. As much as I love the church, I must confess that churches are notorious for being small-minded, faithless, shortsighted, hypocritical (and that says nothing about the times the church has burned people at the stake because they held what were considered unacceptable beliefs). There is an old medieval comparison of the church to Noah's ark: if it were not for the storm raging outside, we could not stand the smell inside.

> "The church is not abandoned to carry out this mission alone; Christ walks among the lampstands."—Boring, *Revelation,* Interpretation, 85.

It is precisely in this environment that Jesus Christ appears:

> But this procedure should be no surprise by now: the site of his birth was a manger, and the palace of his coronation was a cross. God deliberately set Jesus among the common and the flawed—the historical situation just as it was. Jesus is never known in other context. The

revelation of Jesus Christ is not embarrassed or compromised by the association with the church; quite the contrary, it insists on this context. (Peterson, 33)

The sky in which our rainbow—our vision of Christ—is set is the environment of the church. To look elsewhere for Christ is to hold one's head down and not look up to the sky for a rainbow.

Son of Man

The first color of the rainbow, this vision of Christ, is the phrase "as one like a son of man" (RSV; "a human being," NRSV). This phrase "as one like a son of man" is very particular and very clear. Just as the color red is not to be confused with the color green, so this term has a very specific reference. It refers to an Old Testament vision in the book of Daniel of a human figure to whom God will grant everlasting rule.

> I saw in the night visions,
> and behold, with the clouds of heaven
>   there came one like a son of man,
> and he came to the Ancient of Days
>   and was presented before him.
> And to him was given dominion
>   and glory and kingdom,
> that all peoples, nations, and languages
>   should serve him;
> his dominion is an everlasting dominion,
>   which shall not pass away,
> and his kingdom one
>   that shall not be destroyed.
>
> (Daniel 7:13–14, RSV)

Now unless you know this Old Testament reference, you would be color-blind to part of the vision of Christ. One of the Old Testament expectations is the hope of "one like a son of man" who will come as God's representative and rule with justice and peace.

The phrase "son of man" in the context of Daniel simply means a "human being." In fact, it is used elsewhere in the Old Testament as just another way to say "person." For example, the prophet Ezekiel refers to himself frequently as "son of man" and he means no more than "human being."

Jesus himself used this title "Son of Man." People who heard him use it could well have said that he simply refers to himself as "human being." But it always echoed that one Old Testament reference of "one like a son of man," to whom God will give everlasting rule. Jesus' use of the phrase was ambiguous; he was a human being, perhaps more. John's vision touches on that "more."

"The heavenly Christ is no absentee landlord."—Wilfrid J. Harrington, ed., *Revelation*, Sacra Pagina (Collegeville, Minn.: Liturgical Press, 1993), 52.

But where was this more—this powerful Superman—to set straight the evil empires of the world? Where was his dominion with the lightning flashes and the thundering of power? The Son of Man Jesus hung pierced and bleeding on a cross. The one who had dominion and power ate dinner with call girls, had lunch with criminals, wasted time with children, and angered the rich and influential, the pious and godly. Jesus brought together the most glorious title of the Old Testament with the most menial of life styles in the culture. He talked like a king, and lived like a vagrant.

The task of faith for his disciples was to put their confidence in him, to believe that he was the Son of Man through his life of service and sacrificial death. As it was difficult for the disciples to see it, so it was difficult for those to whom John was writing to see. The danger for John's readers is that they will forget that Jesus indeed is the Son of Man. The great danger for them was that life will pound out of them any confidence that Jesus is the Son of Man, the one to whom has been given the dominion, power, and glory.

It is like that riveting scene from the miniseries *Roots,* where the African slave Kunta Kinte has his name whipped out of him. Kunta wants to keep his African name; it is his heritage and birthright. His name marks him as free man. The overseer wants Kunta to submit to the rules of slavery and to forget about trying to escape. One of the ways to enforce this submission is to have Kunta give up his African name and take the name "Toby," which was given by the master.

The overseer flogs Kunta with a whip, asking him, "What's your name?" And after each lash of the whip, the African says, "My name is Kunta." But over and over again the whip cuts into his back until in response to the question, "What's your name?" he says, "My name is Toby."

The danger is that the world will whip us to the point that we no longer can say with confidence that Jesus is Lord, that Jesus has dominion and power and glory. It can be pounded out of us. So it is that John's vision of Jesus begins with this description: "one like a son of man" stands among the churches. In a time of persecution and trial, when the writer himself has been banished from his home because of his Christian faith, it is that sort of vision that is needed.

> "The hand of Christ is strong enough to uphold the heavens and gentle enough to wipe away our tears."—Barclay, *The Revelation of John,* vol. 1, Daily Study Bible, 50.

Priestly Garments

"Son of Man" is one color in the rainbow vision. But there is much more. When we meet someone, we generally notice clothing. Jesus' clothing—a long robe with golden girdle round his breast—is a clear allusion from the Old Testament to priestly apparel (see Ex. 28:4; 29:5: the clothing of Aaron, the high priest). Indeed, the word here for "robe" is used only once in the New Testament but is found seven times in the Greek Old Testament (LXX), and six of these occurrences refer to the attire of the high priest (Mounce, 78).

Like the clerical collar that many ministers wear, which identifies their vocation, so also is the clothing of John's guide. Jesus is dressed as a priest: one who represents us to God, one who represents God to us. He is the bridge between us and God.

John the Seer is playing a priestly role as well in assuring his readers of the presence of Christ in their midst. It is like the story that Martin Luther King Jr. told about Mother Pollard, whose priestly role assured him of the intercession and oversight of God. After a particularly difficult day during the civil rights struggle, Mother Pollard spoke to Rev. King. Sensing that he was afraid, she assured him that the people were with him, and that even if they weren't, God would still take care of him. In King's recollection, at the hearing of her words, his whole body quickened and pulsed with renewed energy (King, 237). John speaks a quickening word to his pastoral charge. Jesus the priest is with them, representing them to God and representing God to us.

The Description of Christ

Once we have noticed what someone is wearing, most us then note physical features, particularly the hair. John's vision of Jesus is that his hair is as white as wool, white as snow. From our Old Testament palette of colors, this description of Jesus signifies his purity. As Isaiah puts it, "Though your sins are like scarlet, they shall be like snow; though they are red like crimson, they shall become like wool" (Isa. 1:18; see also the penitential Psalm 51: ". . . wash me, and I shall be whiter than snow," v. 7; as well as Dan. 7:9). His hair is a sign of overcoming sin, of the victory he has accomplished.

Want to Know More?

About Jewish worship? See Arthur J. Magida, ed., *How to Be a Perfect Stranger*, vol. 1: *A Guide to Etiquette in Other People's Religious Ceremonies* (Woodstock, Vt.: Jewish Lights Publishing, 1996), 211–47.

About the phrase "Son of Man"? See Robert H. Stein, *The Method and Message of Jesus' Teachings*, rev. ed. (Louisville, Ky.: Westminster John Knox Press, 1994), 135–51.

About the number seven and other numbers? See Leland Ryken, James C. Wilhoit, and Tremper Longman III, eds., *Dictionary of Biblical Imagery* (Downers Grove, Ill.: InterVarsity Press, 1998), 599–600.

And the eyes are a "flame of fire." A burning bush, pillars of fire, altar fire, fiery chariots, refining fire, a fiery furnace: the revelatory significance of fire carries throughout the Old Testament. The metaphor of "fiery eyes" suggests that Jesus does not look at us; he looks into us. In St. Andrews, Scotland, they speak of a lazy wind as one that is too lazy to go around you and thus decides to go through you, chilling you to the bone. Jesus' eyes are flame; they do not rest on us, but rather they bore into us.

His feet of burnished bronze are likely a comparative reference to the great statue of Daniel 2 with its "feet of clay." Burnished bronze would thus refer to stability and endurance (see also the description of the angel who guides Daniel, 10:6). Bronze is a combination of iron and copper. Iron is strong, but rusts. Copper does not rust, but is a relatively soft metal. Bronze, the combination, brings together both attributes: the best of both strength and durability.

The voice of Jesus, the guide to John's vision, sounds like many waters. This is the sound of the glory of God (the Shekinah) that returns to inhabit the restored Jerusalem and Temple (Ezek. 43:2). In addition, it is important to remember that John was exiled to a small island, where the sound of waves—the awesome power of the sea—surrounded him. Jesus speaks in a cacophony of sound that is full of meaning.

In his right hand, he has seven stars. We best get used to sevens in the book of Revelation. Series of seven repeat themselves. First, note that numbers appeal to our sense of touch: we can count it on our fingers; we can hold up seven fingers without too much thought or calculation. And as for the number seven itself, what made it so significant?

The reference to seven *stars* points us in one direction: toward the night skies. Before the day of electric lights and evening entertainment such as television, one of the most familiar sights was looking up into the sky on a clear evening to see the myriad of stars, the Milky Way, the dark blue backdrop for the twinkling points of light.

Studying the stars was one of the first human investigations and fascinations. There were seven celestial bodies that were thought to have a motion of their own among the fixed stars: the Sun, the Moon, Venus, Jupiter, Mars, Mercury, and Saturn. Other points of light were found generally in the same place in the sky, but the seven largest points of light moved on their own courses. Seven was written in the sky: the seven largest celestial bodies that moved their own way through the night sky. And, instead of the seven stars controlling the fate of human beings, Jesus, in John's vision, holds seven stars in his hand. The universe seen in the night sky is in Jesus' control.

> **Lucky number 7**
>
> Besides the seven churches, letters, seals, trumpets, and bowls, there are seven "beatitudes" (1:3; 14:13; 16:15; 19:9; 20:6; 22:7,14), seven praise qualities in 5:12, seven references to the altar (6:9; 8:3; 5; 9:13; 11:1; 14:18; 16:7), seven references to the coming Jesus (2:16; 3:11; 16:15; 22:7, 12, 17, 20), and seven visions of Christ (here, 1:12–16; 5:5–6; 12:1–6; 14:1, 14; 19:16; and 22:12–17). Even this vision of Christ can be separated into seven descriptors: white head, eyes, feet, voice, right hand, mouth, and shining face.

Even Jesus' mouth bespeaks the control: like a two-edged sword was his mouth. This image, repeated in 2:16, and in 19:15, 21 (on the return of Christ), connotes judgment, both in Revelation and similar references (see Isa. 49:2, Wisd. Sol. 18:15–16, and Heb. 4:12–13). We may claim that sticks and stones may break our bones, but words will never hurt us, but that is a lie. Words can cut through us, can touch feelings in us that we may wish to ignore or to cultivate. The Jesus that John sees is one whose words cut like a two-edged sword. A two-edged sword was made for thrusting (not for slashing like a saber). Like the flaming eyes that saw into us, his mouth speaks words that are meant to cut into us.

The final aspect of the vision of Jesus is his face. Like the face of Moses, who came down from Mount Sinai with a glow on his countenance that bedazzled the children of Israel, so Jesus' face shines (Ex. 34:29). And the function of light is twofold. The first is to bring out the beautiful and the right, like the function of spotlights on church

> "The giver of light is Jesus Christ. . . . The Christian's light is always a borrowed light."—Barclay, *The Revelation of John*, vol. 1, Daily Study Bible, 53.

buildings and monuments. But light also has another function: to search out what is wrong, as the spotlight on a police cruiser is used to illumine possible criminal activity that may occur in the dark of night. The light brings out the best and the worst.

The Living One

The vision is now complete; we have looked at each component. We have unwoven the rainbow, looking at each specific color. But what of the total effect? What does the vision do? To an exiled, weary Christian, to whom the power of Rome looks insurmountable, the vision gives purpose and meaning.

The difference between John, the exiled prisoner, and John, the pastor, is Christ, in vision and reality.

> St. John, away from his churches, fretting from lack of intimate knowledge of his peoples, sees the penetrating, attentive eyes of his Savior. St. John, weak from confinement, sees the strong, burnished feet of his Lord. St. John, used to speaking with authority to his apt-to-stray sheep but now without a voice, hears the authoritative voice of the Ruler of church and world. St. John, homesick for his congregations, sees them held in the right hand of the Shepherd of Israel. St. John, at the mercy of the political sword of Rome, sees the word of God proceeding swordlike and not returning void. St. John, nearing the end of his days, the energy of his countenance in eclipse, sees the presence of a radiating Christ throwing blessing on all. (Peterson, 41)

The vision—the revelation of Jesus Christ—brings hope and sustains reality.

? Questions for Reflection

1. This unit probes the description of Christ in Revelation 1:12–20. Each generation has its idea of what Christ must be like, seen even in the current interest in the phrase "What Would Jesus Do?" How would you describe Christ? Does the description from this passage fit your idea? Why or why not?
2. John's audience was a church struggling to keep the faith in the face of persecution and suffering. What issues test our faith today?

Are there ways in which John's vision of Christ can help in the struggle? How?

3. Numbers play an important role in the Bible. What are some other biblical stories where numbers give important details? Using a concordance, what are some of the other references in scripture to the number seven? What do you think John was hoping to communicate in his use of this number?

4. The one who stands among the lampstands holds the keys to Death and Hades in his hand. Does this image suggest a message of doom or hope? Why do you think so?

3 Revelation 2–3

Of Angels and Churches

The "letters to the seven churches" (Rev. 2:1–3:22) highlight the pastoral task of the seer John. His vision of the risen Christ is not a private ecstasy but has profound and practical implications for the congregations he knows and loves in the Roman province of Asia. The choice of seven congregations among the many existing congregations in Asia is symbolic of the completeness and fullness of the number seven. The seven messages, as we will note below, address specific, local situations as well as the faith of all congregations.

Because of the similarity in the form and the content of the seven letters and because there is no indication that they were ever delivered separately, there is a broad and cumulative focus of the messages. We will look first at the broad focus. Then, in the next unit, we will examine each letter individually.

Boring (86–91) suggests that the letters share a similar format and content:

1. Address to an angel
2. Name of a city
3. Prophetic messenger formula
4. Christological ascription
5. Divine knowledge ("I know . . . ")
6. Body of letter: affirmation and correction
7. Universal call to listen and obey ("Let anyone who has an ear . . . ")
8. Eschatological promise to those who conquer

Address to an Angel

Although we tend to think of angels in individual terms (and there is much in our popular culture that emphasizes this aspect), John has both an individual and corporate understanding of angels, where angels represent a body of people. In the book of Daniel, which is major influence on the seer's expression, Michael is the guardian angel of Israel (Dan. 10:13, 21; 12:1). In addition, other nations are similarly equipped (Dan. 10:20) with a representative angel. Such a corporate understanding of angels continues in later rabbinic reflections.

Here, in the messages to the seven churches, the risen Christ addresses the angel, who is the corporate representative of the congregation. We can give a modern twist to this corporate understanding by speaking of the personality of a congregation. Congregations, indeed even communities and other institutions, have a history and way of being that is larger than the individuals who are involved. Modern management and leadership studies speak of the culture and spirit of a corporation. The seer John, through the words of Jesus, addresses the personality of the community.

A fascinating, imaginative exercise for pastors or lay leaders to undertake is to write a letter to the "angel" of your particular congregation. In line with the letters to the seven congregations here in Revelation, the question to guide the content of the letter is: "What do you hear God saying in affirmation, correction, and promise to your community?" Such a letter demands knowledge of the history of the congregation, of the present circumstances of congregation and community, and an informed anticipation of the future.

Name of the City

The order of the seven churches forms a circular route that begins in Ephesus, likely following a Roman postal route. The revelation of Jesus Christ, though it has universal application, still addresses local needs and concerns. The now-deceased Speaker of the U.S. House of Representatives Thomas P. ("Tip") O'Neill was often credited with saying that "All politics are local." In other words, no matter how big the issue, politics came down to one neighbor speaking to another, one coworker addressing another, one shopper striking up a conversation with another. The same may be said of the grand words of Jesus: they speak locally.

> "The church is more than a human 'worthy cause'; it participates in the reality of the eternal world."—Boring, *Revelation,* Interpretation, 86.

Prophetic Messenger Formula

The letters to the seven churches follow the format of prophetic speech, particularly exemplified in the Old Testament. In this form of prophetic expression, the prophet gives voice to the direct speech of the Lord (first-person expression with "I," "me," and "mine") and the clincher: "Thus says the Lord." In the ancient Greek translation of the Hebrew Bible, completed centuries before the Christian era, the prophetic conclusion—"says the Lord"—was rendered "the words of the Lord." John, the prophetic seer, writing in Greek, adopts this pattern of speech in each of the letters with the phrase "the words of him who . . ."

John adopts the prophetic speech pattern as the "Lord" speaks through him. As is typical of the entire New Testament, the "Lord" is Jesus. In Jesus' resurrection, he has assumed the role of Lord: "Therefore God also highly exalted him and gave him the name that is above every name . . . Jesus Christ is Lord" (Phil. 2:9–11).

In a red-letter edition of the Bible, where the words of Jesus are put in red letters, the messages to the seven churches are set in red type. This typesetting puts the letters to the seven churches on the same level as words spoken by Jesus of Nazareth: the golden rule, the parables, and so forth. All are words of Jesus.

There is a certain tendency to elevate the words of Jesus expressed in the Gospels as the "real" words of Jesus. In fact, there is a whole line of scholarship that tries to identify what Jesus actually said and what the church said in Jesus' name. The underlying presumption is that the real words of Jesus are the most important, the most genuine, the most authoritative. The words of seer John here in Revelation make no pretense to be the words of the historical Jesus, but they are nevertheless "words of the Lord." To be sure, the seer John uses the prophetic speech pattern and follows the rules of such a speech pattern. He is not transcribing a tape recording of the voice of the risen Christ. We nevertheless have words of the Lord Jesus Christ.

 Want to Know More?

About angels? Joel B. Green, Scot Mc-Knight, I. Howard Marshall, eds., *Dictionary of Jesus and the Gospels* (Downers Grove, Ill.: InterVarsity Press, 1992), 8–11; Gerald F. Hawthorne, Ralph P. Martin, Daniel G. Reid, eds., *Dictionary of Paul and His Letters* (Downers Grove, Ill.: InterVarsity Press, 1993), 20–23.

About Old Testament prophecy? See Celia Brewer Marshall, *A Guide through the Old Testament* (Louisville, Ky.: Westminster John Knox Press, 1989), 87–121.

About visions? See Leland Ryken, James C. Wilhoit, and Tremper Longman III, eds. *Dictionary of Biblical Imagery* (Downers Grove, Ill.: InterVarsity Press, 1998), 217–19.

Christological Ascription

Each church is located geographically by a city, but its identity is defined by its relationship to the risen Christ. Its identity is defined by the Christ, who has been revealed to the seer. Most every element of the Christ vision in 1:12–20 appears again in the letters, with additional details identifying the risen Christ drawn from the local situation that is being addressed or from the overall theology of the seer (see Boring, 88). It is not just a matter of where are you from but whom you are connected with. The recipients are more than residents of particular cities. They are the Lord's (which is the meaning of *kyriakos,* "church").

In a somewhat similar fashion, Paul writes to the "saints" who happen to reside in Corinth, Rome, Galatia, and so forth. The larger category is the saints of God, which defines their identity theologically. The recipients of the seven letters find that their identity is wrapped up in the One who stands among them.

Divine Knowledge

In each message, the Lord Christ speaks as one who knows what is happening in each congregation. This knowledge is, of course, mediated through John, whose pastoral charge is the churches of Asia. The vision of Jesus that precedes the letters places the Lord in the midst of the seven lampstands, the seven churches. He is not removed from their situation.

The biblical concept of knowledge is a rich one. Physical intimacy between a man and woman is a form of knowing (e.g., Matt. 1:25; Luke 1:34, RSV). God's choice of Abraham (Gen. 18:19, RSV) and Abraham's children (Amos 3:2) is a form of knowing. Knowing is a form of empathy: "I know how things are" (see 1 Cor. 2:11; John 21:16). The message of Christ to his churches is that he knows—their troubles, their shortcomings—and they are not forsaken.

"Christians were increasingly faced with a dilemma: to participate in the imperial cult and be regarded as good citizens, or to refuse to participate because the worship of the emperor was another form of idolatry."—C. Freeman Sleeper, *The Victorious Christ*, 42.

"Contrary to the oft-repeated claim that apocalyptic was written by and for deprived, oppressed people who had no political or economic power and were alienated from the larger society, the Revelation to John . . . seems addressed, for the most part, to complacent, spiritually anemic Christians."—Charles H. Talbert, *The Apocalypse*, 25.

Body of the Letter: Affirmation and Correction

The body of each of the letters moves between the two poles of affirmation and correction:

1. An affirmation of the particular expressions of faithfulness of the congregation
2. A word of correction, to discipline the congregation in order to improve faithfulness

Two of the five churches receive no word of affirmation and two of the churches receive no word of correction.

Church	Affirmation	Correction
Ephesus	Vigilant, untiring commitment to right teaching and faithful expressions	Recovering the initial enthusiasm and zest of faith
Smyrna	Brave suffering of poverty and external oppression	NO CORRECTION

Pergamum	Courageous resistance in shadow of evil	Facing the heretical teaching that has been tolerated or ignored
Thyatira	Maturing in faithfulness	Opposing the immorality that is advocated and practiced by a minority
Sardis	NO AFFIRMATION	Awaking from apathy and a false sense of security
Philadelphia	Steadfastness in poverty and powerlessness, but with an opportunity for mission	NO CORRECTION
Laodicea	NO AFFIRMATION	Realizing that the "good life" of luxurious living cannot substitute for the good life of faithfulness

Universal Call to Listen and Obey

Although particular pastoral situations are addressed in each letter, the letters have a more universal application. The repeated refrain in each letter is "Let anyone who has an ear listen to what the Spirit is saying to the churches." Thus what is said to the Christians in Smyrna, for example, applies to all. Indeed, we who look over the shoulders of the original recipients also find that we are addressed by these letters.

Eschatological Promise to Those Who Conquer

In each of the letters, even to those that receive no affirmation, there is a promise. This promise is life—eternal, abundant life—expressed in a variety of images: tree of life in the Paradise of God (Ephesus), crown of life and no "second death" (Smyrna), heavenly food, white stone, and a new name (Pergamum), invincible rule and the morning star (Thyatira), white garments and name in the book of life (Sardis), a pillar in the temple (Philadelphia), and eating and ruling with Christ (Laodicea). As the christological ascription looked back to the Christ vision in 1:12–19, so the promise looks ahead, particularly to the culminating vision of the new heaven and new earth in Revelation 20–22.

The motivating promise of eternal life in all its variety is made to those who conquer. The definition of conquering is set by the risen Christ who speaks the promise. He has conquered through suffering and death. To conquer means to be aligned with him, even following in his suffering footsteps.

"This is an implicit call to follow Jesus' pattern of martyrdom, a call to ultimate human decision."—Boring, *Revelation,* Interpretation, 97.

The power of the promise is in knowing how things will end, come what may. The risen Christ who stands among the lampstands/churches knows not only their present faithfulness and trials but also the future. Knowing the future does not erase the difficulty of the moment, but it does assure the ending. A person going to a dentist for a toothache will not likely be kept from the discomfort of repair, but the assurance of the dentist is: "The pain will be gone, but the steps to reach that stage may be very trying."

"God is just and will ultimately win out over the forces that seek to destroy human life. Without that affirmation, life seems to be chaotic and meaningless."—C. Freeman Sleeper, *The Victorious Christ,* 125.

The letters to the seven churches address particular and time-bound situations at the end of the first century in the Roman province of Asia. However, their message was more universal then, as it is today: "Let anyone with an ear to hear listen to what the Spirit is saying to the churches." The words to the churches are words of affirmation, correction, and promise (Peterson, 53):

- The church is a community that is doing some things right. Holding on is good; loving God and neighbor is blessed. Affirmation plays a role in encouraging and sustaining further expressions of faithfulness.
- The church is the community that is conscious of failing to live up to the legacy of faith and the presence of Christ in its midst. Confession is required; only sinners need apply for membership. Correction plays a role in encouraging and sustaining further expressions of faithfulness.
- The church is the community that lives by the promises. One of the hymns in American gospel music is titled "Standing on the Promises." Promise plays a role in encouraging and sustaining further expressions of faithfulness.

? Questions for Reflection

1. This unit discusses the form, content, and purpose of the seven letters. Think about the other types of literature in the Bible (narrative, proverbs, parables, poetry, etc.). What is different about a letter as compared to those other types of literature? What is the purpose of a letter as compared to the other types? Why are there different types of literature in the Bible? Which type of literature do you prefer? Why?

2. If you were to write a letter to your church, what words of affirmation, correction, and promise might you offer?

3. Most of the letters in these chapters end with the phrase, "the one who conquers." What do you think that means? Why would John be exhorting his hearers to conquer? What would they need to overcome? What might you need to overcome?

4. This unit mentioned the distinction between what might be the actual words of Jesus and the words of the early church spoken in the name of Jesus. What type of issues does this raise for you about the Bible? Why?

4 Revelation 2–3 (Continued)

"I Know Your Works"

The letters to the seven churches are rich in details, images, and themes. In the following, we will take a brief look at highlights of each letter, particularly examining the christological description, the affirmation, correction, and promise in each letter.

The Message to the Church in Ephesus (2:1–7)

The first letter of the risen Christ is to the church in Ephesus. This congregation, at the time of writing, would be a second- and perhaps third-generation congregation. Some forty years have passed since its establishment. (Remember that Paul visited Ephesus, Acts 18:18–21, perhaps in the early 50s.) Although other cities of Asia competed for the title, Ephesus was known as the "first of Asia." It was a major center of sea and land commerce, and it may well have been the port from which John left to enter his political banishment.

The identification of the sender, the risen Christ, is drawn from one of the grandest elements of the vision in 1:12–20. This is the one who controls destiny—the seven stars—and not the one who is controlled by destiny.

The ancient city of Ephesus today

The affirmation of the congregation in Ephesus is twofold. First, its members have worked hard and endured. Their history is good. Second, they have stayed true to the right teaching. They have been orthodox. In the brief history of the early church, Ephesus stands out as a congregation that has aged well. The people have a faithful heritage, and they teach the right things.

This affirmation is tempered by a warning or correction. This congregation is admonished: "You have abandoned the love you had at the first" (2:4). The object of their love is not specified, so that it might include their love for God in Christ as well as their love for one another. A congregation that is apt at walling off false apostles and wayward teaching (the Nicolaitans) may also have the tendency to wall off members from one another. So, the church in Ephesus is like a majestic oak tree whose presence and size may hide a hollowness inside. What has been lost is the enthusiasm, passion, and energy for faithfulness.

The admonition comes with a suggested course of action: to remember and to repent. The remembrance is of their beginnings, the enthusiasm and passion that go with beginnings. The word of the Lord to those in Ephesus is the counsel in the song "Try to Remember," from the musical *The Fantastiks:* If you remember, then follow. The message of Christ is to remember and, secondly, to repent. This repentance is to be marked by doing "the works that you did at first" (2:5).

The motivating promise to this congregation is one of the universal themes of eternal life: the paradisal garden of

> "This is a word that today's church must also heed, for we too may be tempted to set so much store on our correct theology and proper process of church government that we risk forgetting that a church without love is already dead."—González and González, *Revelation,* Westminster Bible Companion, 24.

God. The one who remains steadfast, that is, "the one who conquers," will eat from the tree of life. As always, we need to be careful of overliteralizing any of the images in Revelation, but this last book of the Bible gives us a recapitulation of the first book of the Bible. The first Adam loses the opportunity to eat of the tree of life. Humanity's disobedience to God voids that permission. The new humanity, begun in Christ, is reafforded that opportunity. The second Adam, following a Pauline metaphor for Christ, restores the right to eat from the tree of life to all his brothers and sisters.

The Message to the Church in Smyrna (2:8–11)

The Christ who addresses the congregation in Smyrna is "the first and the last, who was dead and came to life" (2:8). These are strong words for a congregation, whose beginnings were no doubt happy and enthusiastic and whose ultimate future is secure, but who are finding that life "in the middle" between that beginning and the end are very difficult.

This congregation is affirmed for its endurance of both affliction from the outside and poverty. The only possible tinge of correction is found in the phrase "do not fear" (2:10). The affliction appears to be instigated by the Jews of Smyrna. Tragically, the relationship between Christians (even Christian Jews) and Jews had deteriorated greatly by the end of the first century. Jews were distancing themselves from the Christian movement, casting Christians out of their synagogues and going to greater lengths to make it hard on the church. Judaism was well established in the Roman Empire, with special legal status. In part, their motivation for slandering Christians may have been an effort to distinguish themselves from these very suspect Christians. In any case, the more established religious group showed little mercy to the upstart.

One of the ironies of history is that only the city of Smyrna continues to this day. All of the other six cities have passed into oblivion, surviving in memory and as archaeological sites. There is to this day a Christian presence in Izmir (Smyrna). The promise to this congregation was, of course, the "crown of life."

The Message to the Church in Pergamum (2:12–17)

The Christ who addresses the church in Pergamum is the one who has the sharp two-edged sword. This image, drawn from the vision in 1:12–20, stands in strong contrast to the local setting of this church in the city of Pergamum. Pergamum, as the capital of the Roman province of Asia, was the seat of the proconsul who had "the right of the sword" (*ius gladii*). The "right of the sword" was the power to execute at will. Although not explicitly related to this executing power, it is significant that this letter alone praises a martyr by name, a faithful witness named Anitipas who has been killed. The risen Christ, with the two-edged sword, has the real power of over life and death. (Remember the discussion from the previous unit.)

The affirmation of the Pergamum congregation is that it is holding fast, even though they live "where Satan's throne is" (2:13). What made Pergamum like living in the shadow of Satan's throne is not exactly certain, although there are several good possibilities.

> "The church is not spectator to the cosmic battle between God and the forces of evil but experiences it in its own life."—Boring, *Revelation*, Interpretation, 92.

There was a prominent, throne-like temple to Zeus. There was a great temple to the healing god Asclepius, of which a major symbol was a serpent. The "serpent," for anyone with Jewish roots, would ring of the serpent in the garden. However, the greatest shadow of Satanic rule may well be the primacy of the imperial cult in Pergamum. As we will note when we come to Revelation 13, the imperial cult had taken on beastly connotations for John's congregation. The Christians who lived in Pergamum did not live at the battle front. They lived behind enemy lines, where active resistance was futile and the temptation to give up was most powerful.

The congregation, however, is commended for its perseverance. Only some have followed the path of accommodation. Although couched in terms of following "the teaching of Balaam" and "the Nicolaitans," the scholarly consensus about the internal difficulties in the Pergamum church and the other churches is that some are seeking a mediating way between the ethical and purity standards of their faith and the demands of social and economic life. The issue is that at some point accommodation becomes a slippery slope that leads to the complete undermining of faithfulness. The perspective of Revelation is very stark: one is either in or out. The prophetic message, as typically experienced by the

> "Repentance is not a once-and-for-all act that brings one into the Christian community but is the constant challenge to the community."—Boring, *Revelation*, Interpretation, 95–96.

people of faith, is one that questions the accommodation to the status quo and affirms the perseverance to radical and simple faithfulness (see Boring, 92–93).

The motivating promise draws on an ancient tradition and a current practice. The ancient tradition is that of eating the hidden manna. Manna was the heavenly food that fed the people of God in their wanderings in the wilderness. The manna that is hidden is probably a reference to the manna that was stored in the Ark of the

Covenant (Ex. 16:33–34). According to Jewish tradition (2 Macc. 2:1ff.), the Ark was hidden until the Messianic Age.

Along with this ancient image that symbolizes inclusion in the people of God, there is the promise of receiving a white stone. Although there are a dozen or more suggestions about what this white stone is, most of them have something to do with admission and inclusion. For example, a special stone might be issued as ticket to get into a feast at a temple. The faithful have a better opportunity; they will have a ticket for the supper of the Messiah.

The Message to the Church in Thyatira (2:18–29)

The description of the risen Christ who addresses this congregation is couched in terms from the vision of 1:12–16—flaming eyes and burnished bronze feet—as well as a new element. The new element is the title "Son of God," which is connected with the allusion to Psalm 2 in 2:26–27. Psalm 2, especially verse 7, was utilized by the early church in proclaiming its faith in Jesus' messiahship and divine enthronement at his resurrection from the dead (Acts 4:25–26; 13:33; Heb. 1:5; 5:5).

The affirmation of the congregation commends the people for their "love, faith, service, and faithful endurance." The first two descriptors note the internal qualities, love and faith, which undergird the results that follow—the working out of these internal qualities in ministry and patience. In contrast to the congregation in Ephesus, which has retreated from its "first love," this congregation in Thyatira has matured. The affirmation highlights the development and growth in the things that matter: love, faith, service, and patient endurance.

The correction needed by this congregation is expressed in Old Testament imagery. A woman, someone like Jezebel in the Old Testament (1 Kings 16:29ff.; 2 Kings 9:30ff.), is undercutting the faith of God's people. The issue appears to be accommodation, particularly in terms of fornication and meat offered to idols. The term "fornication" may have literal, sexual overtones, since pagan feasts and practices often led to sexual promiscuity (see Mounce, 104). However, the Old Testament precedent for such language points toward religious infidelity (e.g., Hos. 9:1; Jer. 3:6; Ezek. 23:19).

The details of the accommodation and compromise advocated by Jezebel and the Nicolaitans are not clear. However, the issue is faced by every generation of the church: "How much do we adopt the contemporary standards and mores of the culture in which we live?" Superior knowledge (note the irony in the phrase "the deep things of Satan") is overwhelming the central ethical focus of the faith. As with the warning to the church in Pergamum, there is no compromise with those who compromise the faith. Again, the level of conflict in the rhetoric reflects the crisis that threatens the church.

The promise accorded the church in Thyatira is a free rendering of Psalm 2:8–9, foreshadowed by the term "Son of God" in the opening, christological description. The strident language of conquering is filled out; the disciples of the ruling shepherd will rule and shepherd with him. The sharing in the rule of Christ contrasts the lack of rule that the Thyatiran congregation is experiencing. This feature of sharing in the rule of the Messiah is part of Jewish expectation and Christian expectation (e.g., Matt. 11:28; 1 Cor. 6:3; Rev. 5:10).

The Message to the Church in Sardis (3:1–6)

The Christ who speaks to the congregation in Sardis is the one "who has the seven spirits of God and the seven stars" (3:1). The seven stars, representing the seven churches (1:20), represent the totality of the church. Likewise, although enigmatic for us, the seven spirits represent the totality of the Holy Spirit.

A thought-construct foreign to our thought is the Semitic plural of intensity or "abstract plural." For example, the standard word for "God" in the Old Testament is *elohim,* which is a plural. It is used repeatedly where the word "gods" is intended and repeatedly where the word "God" is intended. It is the same word. Translators must make the judgment as to whether the context demand "gods" (plural and with a little "g") or "God" (singular and with a capital "G"). When used for "God," this plural form corresponds to our word "Godhead" or "divinity" and is suited to the task of summing up the divine power in a personal unity (Eichrodt, 185–87).

The "seven spirits" likely fits this type of expression: a plural of intensity or "abstract plural." The totality of the Spirit is what is needed in the Sardis congregation. Its members receive only correction and no affirmation. The Sardis church has the reputation of being alive, but is really dead. The risen Christ sounds the wake-up call for a church that is in the slumbers of death. This congregation needs the total work of the life-giving Spirit.

As many commentators have noted, the falling asleep metaphor leading up to death would be a very live metaphor for the Sardis community. The city of Sardis was built on an acropolis that was virtually inaccessible from all directions save one: the south. The other directions looked out over a nearly perpendicular cliff that fell away about fifteen hundred feet to the lower valley. This natural citadel, however, was twice conquered during wars because the residents only guarded the southern access. Each defeat was due to a few intrepid, enemy soldiers working their way up the cliffs and securing the city gates. Sardis's defenders were not vigilant of the cliffs. They were not awake to the danger, and it meant the city's doom.

> "As one looks around, one sees many churches where there is a semblance of life, a sort of 'coasting' on past glories and achievements, the sort of assurance that the sentinels on the wall of Sardis must have felt before the city was taken by the enemy. There is nothing wrong with such churches. And yet, everything is wrong with them!"—González and González, *Revelation*, Westminster Bible Companion, 33.

The congregation is urgently called to waken lest Christ come like a thief: a visitation to be avoided by vigilance, by repentance, and by a return to former ways. Like the churches in Ephesus, Pergamum, and (later) Laodicea, repentance is the means of renewal. Like the prodigal son of whom the Father said, "This my son of mine was dead" (Luke 15:22), so the Sardis congregation had the opportunity for life in repentance and return.

Even though this congregation receives no commendation, there is still a minority of members who are faithful, who have not "soiled their clothes" and who will be dressed in white. Part of the motivating promise is that all will be so dressed, pending their continued faithfulness. Indeed, their names will be kept in the "book of life."

White garments or robes are mentioned seven times (3:5, 18; 4:4; 6:11; 7:9, 13; 19:14)—further evidence of John's literary skill. White is a sign of purity, but it also would ring of parade colors. The Roman tradition was to wear white on days of triumph, celebrating victory. Those who conquer will be fitted out in purity and in triumph.

The image of a ledger, the "book of life," has both biblical and secular antecedents. In the Old Testament, the "book of life" is the register of all who have a place among the saints of God (see Ex. 32:32–33; Ps. 69:28; Dan. 12:1). In addition, like the voting roll kept by cities and counties, there would be a civic register in each of these cities in Asia. Exclusion from that register would mean exclusion from economic and political rights.

The message to the sleepy church of Sardis is stark. Like the letter to Laodicea, its harsh tone is set in the context of wanting the best for the congregation: "I reprove and discipline those whom I love. Be earnest, therefore, and repent" (3:19).

The Message to the Church at Philadelphia (3:7–13)

The christological description that opens this letter branches out beyond the vision of Christ in 1:12–20. Although keys are mentioned in 1:19, there they are the keys of Death and Hades and here it is the "key of David." The key and the authority to open and shut are allusions to Isaiah 22:15–25, where Eliakim, the servant of Hezekiah, is given full run of the royal household: "I will place on his shoulder the key of the house of David; he shall open, and no one shall shut; he shall shut, and no one shall open" (Isa. 22:22; see Rev. 3:7). The key of David leads toward the body of the text that anticipates inclusion in the new Jerusalem (the city of David) and addresses the practice of the local synagogue in casting out Christian Jews.

> ### The Book of Life
>
> References or allusions to the book of life appear throughout scripture (see Ex. 32:32 and Phil. 4:3 among others). This image is both an exhortation to persevere, and a guarantee to the faithful that their reservations have been made in the house of the Lord forever.

The church in Philadelphia, like the church in Smyrna, receives only affirmation and no correction. The risen Christ sees that though the Philadelphian congregation has little power and influence, it has a great opportunity for mission. The church is faithfully taking on this mission. Playing off the door imagery, this church has an open door for mission. The metaphor of an open door is used by Paul to describe mission opportunity (1 Cor. 16:9; compare 2 Cor. 2:12; Col. 4:3). Geographically, Philadelphia was well situated on trade routes. It was known as the "gateway to the East" (eastern Asia Minor and beyond). Here was a door for mission, even for a small congregation.

The difficulty for the church in Philadelphia does not appear to come from pagan pressures but rather from the synagogue. Again, as in Smyrna, the first-century conflict between the Christian movement and established Judaism is evident. All too often, the established group oppresses the minority upstart. Church anti-Semitism in later centuries will attest to this.

The risen Christ promises that the faithful endurance of the Philadelphians will stand them in good stead: "Because you have kept my word of patient endurance, I will keep you from the hour of trial that is coming on the whole world to test the inhabitants of the earth" (3:10). Although it is very literally said "keep you from the hour of trial," the underlying Greek can be read as "keep you through the hour of trial." In other words, the promise is that the risen Christ will see them through the inevitable trials that they too will experience. This congregation will not somehow be exempted from trouble.

The motivating promise to the church of Philadelphia connects to a later image in the book of Revelation, that of the new Jerusalem (21:1ff.). Again, the fluidity of meta-phors is evident; the promise is that they will be pillars in the temple of God, al-though later the new Jerusalem is specif-ically characterized as having "no temple" (21:22). The pillar metaphor—secure, stable, holding up—is a familiar meta-phor (See Gal. 2:9; 1 Tim. 3:15). This imagery, in the context of first-century Philadelphia, would have sev-eral connections. First, the city of Philadelphia was severely damaged by an earthquake in 17 C.E. (Common Era or "A.D."). The promise is to be a stable fixture in the new Jerusalem, from which there would be no need to flee because of an earthquake. Second, Philadelphia (like the other cities) had multiple temples, recognized places of worship. To the Christian community that had no recognized place of worship, the promise to be a part of the new Temple in the new Jerusalem assuages that longing for a place. As is typical of the New Testament, here build-ing imagery is used to describe the church. The church is the "build-ing" of people and not a structure, a distinction often lost in our use of the word "church" to refer to an actual building.

> "The Christian life . . . is not adherence to moralistic norms but a life lived in view of the reality of the Christ event in the past and the victory of God in the . . . future."
> —Boring, *Revelation*, Interpretation, 89.

The Message to the Church at Laodicea (3:14–22)

The seventh message comes from the one who is "the Amen, the faithful and true witness, the origin of God's creation" (3:14). This description departs from the vision of 1:12–20. Describing someone as "Amen" is rare in scripture. Only translating Isaiah 65:16 as "the God of Amen" ("of faithfulness" in the NRSV) would be the other instance. "Amen" means "truth"; it has been brought into the church's language as a liturgical con-clusion, usually to acknowledge the validity of what has preceded.

The reference to "origin of God's creation" is reminiscent of Colossians 1:15, which speaks of Christ as "the firstborn of all creation." Maybe there is an intended allusion to ending ("Amen") and beginning ("origin"). Sandwiched between this ending and beginning is a reference to "the faithful and true witness" (3:14). The Greek word used here for "witness" is the root of our word "martyr." This opening to the letter may be suggesting that life in the middle of that ending and beginning calls for faithful and true service even to death, a striking contrast to life in the church in Laodicea.

The final message of the risen Christ is to a church in the wealthiest city of the region of Phrygia. The elements of local color that appear in this letter are readily apparent. Laodicea was a major banking center (a dealer in gold), a major medical center (particularly known for its eye salve), and a clothing center (a soft, glossy black wool was used in a variety of garments). The word of the Lord to them is that despite their banks overflowing in gold, they are poor; despite their doctors and eye medications, they are blind; despite their production of fine clothing, they are naked.

This congregation, like that of Sardis, receives no affirmation and only correction. The barrenness of the faithfulness of the church of Laodicea revolves around its perception of its own self-sufficiency. This church was located in a city that refused Roman help after a disastrous earthquake some thirty years earlier. Laodiceans take care of themselves—they have no need of the Roman Empire's equivalent of the Federal Emergency Management Agency (FEMA). With that self-sufficiency, complacency has set in; they are "lukewarm."

 Want to Know More?

About the letters to the seven churches? See M. Eugene Boring, *Revelation*, Interpretation, 85–97. For a thorough history of interpretation, see Robert H. Mounce, *The Book of Revelation* (Grand Rapids: Wm. B. Eerdmans Publishing Co., 1977).

About the Nicolaitans? See Boring, *Revelation*, Interpretation, 92–93.

About perseverance and endurance? See Shirley C. Guthrie, *Christian Doctrine*, rev. ed. (Louisville, Ky.: Westminster John Knox Press, 1994), 189–90.

About fear? See William Barclay, *New Testament Words* (Philadelphia: Westminster Press, 1976), 227–32.

About manna? See Paul J. Achtemeier, ed., *Harper's Bible Dictionary* (San Francisco: Harper & Row, 1985), 600–601.

About the Tree of Life? See Leland Ryken, James C. Wilhoit, and Tremper Longman III, eds., *Dictionary of Bibical Imagery* (Downers Grove, Ill.: InterVarsity Press, 1998), 889–90.

The image of lukewarm water to be spit out is one of the most memorable metaphors in the seven letters. Again, local color makes it more understandable. The major weakness of the city of Laodicea was water. The closest water source was undrinkable because of its mineral content and its temperature. Water flowed from hot springs at the nearby city of Hierapolis across a plain and then spilled over a cliff that was just north of the city of Laodicea. Near Laodicea, this water was lime- and sulfur-filled and lukewarm, to be spit out, should anyone take a drink.

The contrasting adjectives "hot," "cold," and "lukewarm" are not references to spiritual fever or lack thereof. The two nearby cities of Colossae and Hierapolis provide the context. Hierapolis was known for its hot springs, therapeutically valued. Colassae was known for its cold, pure water. What is found wanting in Laodicea is "useful" water. What is found wanting in the Laodicean congregation is their effective work, not their spiritual temperature. The desire for them to be "cold"—effective and useful—is the same as the desire for them to be "hot."

After such a rigorous correction, the surprising turn is the warmth and gentleness of the motivating promise. The vividness of

the metaphor of lukewarm water being spit out is matched by the image of Christ standing at the door and knocking. Although Revelation 3:20 is often used in revival settings, addressing those outside or estranged from the faith, these words are initially and most aptly addressed to insiders. And, although there is no direct allusion to the celebration of the Lord's Supper, it is hard to imagine how this metaphor would not be taken as a reference to this meal. This is a congregation, already established in the mid-fifties, which would have had decades of observances of the Lord's Supper. Renewed faithfulness by the Laodicean congregation will lead to the presence of Christ, not as a visitation for punishment, but as a visitation of communion and fellowship.

The concluding promise to the Laodicean congregation is an apt conclusion to the entire series of letters. The Christ who stands in their midst comes not just for judgment or for final victory. He comes for spiritual fellowship with believers in worship. This is a word of the Lord for all the churches. "Let anyone who has an ear listen to what the Spirit is saying to the churches."

? Questions for Reflection

1. Christ accuses the church at Ephesus with, "I have this against you, that you have abandoned the love you had at first" (2:4). What do you think this might mean? What is the love that the Ephesian church has left behind? How might this have happened? Keeping this accusation in mind, what word of caution is there for us today?
2. According to this unit, the charge against the church at Pergamum is that its members have accommodated their faith to their surroundings. How does one live in today's pluralistic society while affirming one's faith? What are the central beliefs of your faith that cannot be compromised?
3. The exhortation to the church at Sardis is to "wake up" (3:2), calling to mind Jesus' plea in the garden with his disciples (Mark 14:34). To what should the faithful be awake? How does one stay awake spiritually?
4. "I am rich, I have prospered, and I need nothing" (3:17). Contrast this statement with the perspective of Psalm 23, or the beatitude in Matthew 5:3. To those who are affluent, what does the gospel offer?

5 Revelation 4–5

The Heavenly Worship

In the seventh letter to the churches, the prophetic word of the Lord to John, the visionary writer of the book of Revelation, is "Listen! I am standing at the door, knocking; if you hear my voice and open the door, I will come in to you and eat with you, and you with me" (3:20). Then two sentences later John writes: "After this I looked, and there in heaven a door stood open!" (4:1).

In the first instance, the door is the opening up of the individual to the presence of Christ in worship, particularly at the table of the Lord's Supper. In the second instance, another door is opened, which gives the seer a vision of heaven. What John finds on the other side of the door into heaven is exactly what is happening on earth: worship. John, in the Spirit on the Lord's Day (Sunday) "walks into" or "looks in on" a heavenly worship service. And what he finds in the heavenly worship is simply an expansion of the worship that he experiences. For the heavenly worship involves four actions: centering, gathering, revealing, and singing (Peterson, 57–71).

Centering

What John sees at the center of heaven is the throne of God. It is described with as much brilliance as he, the seer, knows: deep and colorful jewels, light like a rainbow, set on a shimmering sea of glass (perhaps much like the shimmering sea around the island of Patmos at sunset where he, John, was imprisoned). Everything else—the angelic beings, the twenty-four elders, even the singing—points toward the center.

(See Boring, 102–8, for fuller details about the images and their Old Testament background, particularly Ezek. 1:4–28 and Isa. 6:1ff.)

As has often been noted, throne language is a major theme in Revelation (1:8; 4:8; 11:17; 15:3; 16:7, 14; 19:6, 15; 21:22; see 2:13 and 16:10, where the contrasting power of Satan and the beast have a "throne"). Throne language is inherently political language. The political overtones are complemented by the following details (see Boring, 103):

> "In John's vision there is a throneroom for the universe, and the throne is not vacant. The universe is not a chaos nor is it ruled by blind fate. Someone is in charge."
> —Boring, *Revelation*, Interpretation, 102.

1. The repeated "Worthy art thou" (4:11; 5:9, 12) directed to God/Christ reflects the acclamation used to greet the emperor during his triumphal entrance. (This was like saying "Hail Caesar"; a twentieth-century equivalent might be "Heil Hitler.")
2. The title "Lord and God" (4:8) is paralleled by the emperor Domitian's insistence that he be addressed by this title. (Domitian was likely emperor at the time of John's writing.)
3. The twenty-four elders may have multiple meanings (see further below), but Domitian was surrounded by twenty-four lictors (attendants to Roman rulers).
4. The act of the twenty-four elders placing their crowns before God's throne (4:10) is similar to the report by the Roman historian Tacitus of a Parthian king placing his diadem before the image of Nero in order to pay homage.

The throne is at the center of heavenly worship. With careful reverence, John does not describe God who sits on the throne. John's vision is consistent with the words of the hymn: "Immortal, invisible, God only wise, in light inaccessible hid from our eyes." However, the throne is shared by Christ, who is "seen" throughout the book (3:20; 5:13; 7:9, 17; 22:1, 3).

> This language is not intended to conjure up some mental picture of double occupancy of the throne of the universe or of a parceling out of its rule between God and Christ. It is John's way of declaring that the throne of the Lamb and the throne of God are one and the same— God is the one who has defined himself in Jesus Christ; that when Christians say "God," the one they refer to is the one definitively revealed in Jesus, the Crucified. (Boring, 106)

The central focus of the heavenly worship is on the throne of God and the Lamb, as it is for the earthly worship. Worship is a time of centering for John and his communities as it has been for the church through the centuries. Without a center, faith can become like a kite in the wind without the center crosspiece (without the vertical and horizontal sticks). There will be flapping and jerking about in the wind, but no purpose, no potential for flying. But with the center crosspiece, the kite is ready for flying in the wind that would seek to blow it and buffet it about. What John finds in heavenly worship (and what we can conclude about our worship) is that there is a center: the throne of God. In the times of tribulation ahead, worship is centered on God and the Lamb.

"The story begins in heaven—at God's throne. That's where everything begins. That is where the universe began and the stars were flung into space. That is where history begins—and ends."—H. Stephen Shoemaker, *GodStories: New Narratives from Sacred Texts* (Valley Forge, Pa.: Judson Press, 1998), 307.

Gathering

Around that center, there is a gathering (the second aspect of heavenly worship). This gathering is an odd sort for our modern eyes, but comes right out of the Old Testament and the early Christian experience.

First, there are twenty-four elders wearing white robes and golden crowns. The best explanation is that they represent the totality of God's people: twelve patriarchs, representing the twelve tribes of Israel, and twelve apostles, chosen by Jesus as a symbolic "new Israel." A double-twelve: twenty-four. A specific reference to each of these groups is found in the vision of the "new Jerusalem": The names of the twelve tribes are inscribed on the twelve gates of the city and the names of the twelve apostles are on the twelve foundations (21:12–14).

The twenty-four are gathered around the throne of God, representing all of God's people: the Hebrew tribes and the church. They bow to the center throne, taking off their crowns and submitting themselves to God. In doing this, they follow the Roman tradition of submission: when a king surrendered to Rome, there was a ceremony where the king would place his crown before either Caesar in person or a portable image of Caesar. Completing the scene, around the throne was the sea, as of glass. (See Boring, 105, for the multiple associations with "sea.") This scene is captured by Reginald Heber in the hymn "Holy, Holy, Holy":

Holy, holy, holy! all the saints adore Thee,
> Casting down their golden crowns around the glassy sea . . .

Heber characterizes the twenty-four elders as representing the totality of the people of God: all the saints. In other words, heavenly worship is linked to the worship of all the saints, even those on earth. This connection between the heavenly worship and earthly worship is further cemented in the bowl of incense that each elder holds: "the golden bowls full of incense . . . are the prayers of the saints" (5:8). The prayers in earthly worship fill the heavenly worship.

It is not just the representative twenty-four elders who are gathered to the throne, but also the four living creatures, those creatures we would probably connect only with a nightmare:

> Around the throne, and on each side of the throne, are four living creatures, full of eyes in front and behind: the first living creature like a lion, the second living creature like an ox, the third living creature with a face like a human face, and the fourth living creature like a flying eagle. (4:6b–7)

When one adds to this description their six wings, one gets a rather odd sort of a picture: wings, eyes, different faces. But in the Hebrew tradition, both within and outside the Old Testament, these creatures were one of the ways that God's angels were viewed. These four living creatures represent the Hebrew conception of angels: what are called seraphim and cherubim (again, language that Heber used in the hymn "Holy, Holy, Holy").

Looking beyond the oddity of their appearance, the living creatures are representative of all of the animal kingdom: (1) the noblest animal, the king of the beasts: the lion; (2) the strongest animal of the field: the ox; (3) the wisest animal: the human; and (4) the swiftest animal: the eagle. They represent the best of the animal kingdom, all surrounding the throne.

So the impact of John's vision is this: Around the centering throne are the Hebrew tribes, the Christian apostles, the gamut of nature: the king of the beasts, domesticated livestock, human beings, soaring birds. All the created order is gathered around the center. The scene is captured in the hymn attributed to St. Francis of Assisi: "All creatures of our God and King, Lift up your voice and with us sing!" The singing will be addressed after we consider the "revealing."

Revealing

The center draws the gathering for the revealing of God's intention and purpose (the revealing is the third aspect of worship). For in the midst of this glorious gathering, John sees that there is a sealed scroll in the right hand of God of which it is said: "No one in heaven or on earth or under the earth was able to open the scroll or to look into it" (5:3). And when John sees it, he weeps.

John is in the doorway to heaven, experiencing heavenly bliss. And he weeps, all because a scroll cannot be opened. What could that scroll be that is so important, so moving for John? We get the answer when we see who can open the scroll. One of the twenty-four elders guides John: "Do not weep. See, the Lion of the tribe of Judah, the Root of David, has conquered, so that he can open the scroll and its seven seals" (5:5).

Lion of Judah. Root of David. These are images of the Old Testament expectation of the conquering Messiah. The Old Testament Messiah: he is the one who can open the scroll.

> "It seems so right. At the hands of history's evil empires, God's people have been lambs for the slaughter long enough. . . . What we need is God's messiah, full of righteous indignation and God's power, to turn the tables, punish the oppressors, and establish justice. The 'Great Lion of God' is the answer to our prayers (it's about time!) and cause for celebration."—Boring, *Revelation*, Interpretation, 108.

Then, as John prepares for the grand entrance of this figure into the heavenly worship, he sees "a Lamb standing as if it had been slaughtered" (5:6). A reversal occurs here. Instead of a Lion, there is a lamb; instead of a conqueror, one who has been conquered. The elder points toward an Old Testament figure, a royal lion, and what John sees is a lamb. But this is the one who can open the scroll.

Although there will be revelation in the scroll itself (as succeeding chapters of Revelation will indicate), the primary revelation is this transformation in image, this transformation in reality. The Lion is really the Lamb; the real power to conquer is found in the one who stood before Roman authority, was found guilty, and lost his life. But in the higher court, he is fully acquitted and finds life. All revelation begins with this transformation.

In worship the revelation of "what is written" comes through the one who has been proven worthy, who has conquered. How will the church hear the words of the Hebrew scripture that are so lavishly sprinkled through this book? Through the transformed understanding and experience of the lion of Judah, the root of David. Revelation comes through the slain Lamb who has conquered.

In some ways, this entire scene of the Lamb unfolding the written word is like the scene in the Gospel of Luke when Jesus comes home to Nazareth. Jesus worships in the synagogue and is invited to read. He reads from a scroll of the book of Isaiah:

"The Lion of the tribe of Judah"

> The Spirit of the Lord is upon me, because he has anointed me to bring good news to the poor. He has sent me to proclaim release to the captives and recovery of sight to the blind, to let the oppressed go free, to proclaim the year of the Lord's favor. (Luke 4:18–19)

Then Jesus closed the scroll and said: "Today this scripture has been fulfilled in your hearing" (Luke 4:21). The Old Testament was fulfilled in Jesus: today, he said to those in Nazareth, it has been fulfilled in your presence.

Who can open up the Old Testament to the people of God? The lion of Judah, the root of David (Old Testament images of the Messiah). Yes, but the images are turned upside down. It is the Lamb who once was slaughtered that can do the revealing. Worship is the revealing of "what is written" through the Lamb; only the Lamb of God can unseal it and uncover its meaning for us. For only he is worthy to unseal it, and only through him do we uncover the meaning of God found in scripture in our earthly worship. Worship means a center point of God that gathers us together to hear scripture revealed through Christ. The response is to sing!

Singing

In this heavenly worship service in the fourth and fifth chapters of Revelation, there is singing (the fourth aspect of worship). There are five hymns, five songs of praise. The first two are to God, the second two are to Jesus, and the final one is to both.

The first song goes:

> Holy, holy, holy,
>   the Lord God the Almighty,
>   who was and is and is to come.
>   (4:8)

Like the seraphim of Isaiah 6, the threefold "holy" is sung in heavenly worship. The threefold holiness matches a threefold portrayal of God's eternity: "who was, and is, and is to come." This rings of the "I AM WHO I AM" of Exodus 3:14, who was, is, and is to be. The additional wrinkle is that God is not static and distant. God will come. The later vision of Revelation 21 will put it: God will dwell with his people.

The second song continues in praise of God:

> You are worthy, our Lord and God,
>   to receive glory and honor and power,
> for you created all things,
>   and by your will they existed and were created.
>   (4:11)

Want to Know More?

About the images in Revelation 4—the throne room, the sea, the rainbow, etc.? See the excellent discussion in M. Eugene Boring, *Revelation,* Interpretation, 101–7.

About expectations and titles of the Messiah? For a thorough discussion, see George Arthur Buttrick, ed., *The Interpreter's Dictionary of the Bible,* vol. K–Q (Nashville: Abingdon, 1962), 360–65.

About seraphim? See Otto Kaiser, *Isaiah 1–12,* 2d ed., Old Testament Library (Philadelphia: Westminster Press, 1983), 125–26.

Along with the contrast to the acclamation of the emperor Domitian as "worthy" and as "Lord and God," this hymn addresses the work of God in creation. The first hymn emphasized the divine attributes of eternity. This hymn emphasizes the handicraft of God in creation. Even in the midst of the heavenly worship, far removed from the created order, there is no escapism from and no denigration of the earthly. "All things" are from the hand of the worthy God.

The elders and the four living creatures sing a new song to the Lamb:

> You are worthy to take the scroll
>   and to open its seals,
> for you were slaughtered and by your blood you ransomed for God
>   saints from every tribe and language and people and nation;
> you have made them to be a kingdom and priests serving our God,
>   and they will reign on earth.
>   (5:9–10)

The worthiness of God was seen in the act of creation. The worthiness of the Lamb is seen in the act of sacrifice. God creates all things; the Lamb creates the church, the "saints from every tribe and language and people and nation."

The fourth song is also to Jesus:

> Worthy is the Lamb that was slaughtered
> to receive power and wealth and wisdom and might
> and honor and glory and blessing!
>
> (5:12)

Counting the adjectives applied to the Lamb who is worthy, we find our friend seven. Seven adjectives for the Lamb (in a book marked by sevens). This hymn is a shortened version of Phil. 2:6–11: the humbleness of the one who was in the form of God, who took on the identity of a servant, suffering even unto death, leading to exaltation and lordship.

> "Now the chorus of praise goes so far that it cannot go farther, for it reaches throughout the whole of the universe and the whole of creation. There is one vast song of praise to the Lamb."—Barclay, *The Revelation of John*, vol. 1, Daily Study Bible, 180–81.

And then the final hymn is to both God and Jesus:

> To the one seated on the throne and to the Lamb
> be blessing and honor and glory and might
> forever and ever!
>
> (5:13)

This final song wraps up well the vision; the throne of God reminds us that God can do all things: an image of power, might, and strength. The Lamb of God reminds us that God does all things through suffering grace: an image of humility and sacrifice. The throne by itself would be sheer power, before which we would only be blinded and frightened. The lamb alone would be sheer grace, but have no power. What can a little lamb do for you and me? Power and grace together: the throne and the lamb. That is worth singing about!

John's vision of worship is not really bizarre or out of character or even out of touch with reality. Earthly worship is but

> "Crucifixion was not an incident which once happened in the cosmic career of the Messiah and then was superseded by the resurrection and exaltation; it is the definitive act which stamps its character on the identity of the Christ, and is thus definitive for the identity of God. Love was not a provisional strategy of the earthly Jesus, to be eventually replaced by transcendant, eschatological violence when 'they've had their chance' and love has not 'worked.'"—Boring, *Revelation*, Interpretation, 109.

a reflection of the heavenly worship. Evelyn Underhill has written that many a congregation must look "like a muddly, puddly [sea] shore at low tide; littered with every kind of rubbish and odds and ends." That is, we are people who have growled at our spouses or children even as we prepared for worship; we are people who sing hymns off-key; we are people whose minds wander in the hard pews on which we sit. We are muddly, puddly seashore. But then the "tide of worship comes in," Underhill declares, "and it's all gone: the dead sea urchins and jellyfish, the paper and the empty cans and the nameless rubbish. The cleansing sea flows over the whole lot" (Evelyn Underhill, *Collected Papers;* London: Longmans, Green & Co., 1946, p. 78; as cited by Peterson, 71).

Worship is an open door into heaven as we let the sea flow over us: to center us, to gather us, to reveal to us, and to lift us in song. Our prayers are there, and we can join in the hymns. "And the four living creatures said, 'Amen!' And the elders fell down and worshiped" (5:14).

? Questions for Reflection:

1. These chapters describe John's vision of worship in heaven. Many people have trouble with traditional images of heaven, or those encouraged by popular culture and television. If you were to describe heaven, what would it be like? What language and images would you use? Why?

2. It is the Lamb who is worthy (5:9). Why? What does the term "worthy" mean? Compare your definition with that of a dictionary. One of the understandings for the Greek word translated "worthy" is "equal in value." What is it about the Lamb that makes it "equal in value?" To what is the Lamb "equal in value?"

3. This unit suggests four actions of heavenly worship, one being centering. What is the center of the heavenly worship described by John? Think about the worship services you attend most often. What is the center of the service? How do you determine what is the center of a worship service? Should an earthly worship service mirror John's vision of the heavenly worship? Why or why not?

4. There is a reference in the worship scene in 5:8 to incense being the "prayers of the saints." What do you think that means? What kind of prayers do you think these are? Does this include all prayer? People pray for many things—good weather, missions, missing pets, lost jobs, the sick, the embattled—just to name a few. How does thinking about prayer as a component of worship change your feelings about prayer? How does it change your feelings about worship?

The Seals of History

One of the major misreadings of the book of Revelation is to think of it as an almanac, a schedule of upcoming events. The series of seven seals (6:1–17, 8:1–5), then seven trumpets (8:6–11:19), and finally seven bowls (15:5–16:21), have often been mined for the nuggets of the future, typically the near future. Such interpretations have a deterministic bent: suggesting or believing that God will act only according to a very specific plan of action.

In contrast to this chronological reading, we hold to a more poetic interpretation: the series of seven emphasize a unity and not a sequence. "Seven" is used throughout the book to signify wholeness, completeness, and unity: seven churches, seven spirits, seven adjectives for the Lamb, seven "blessings," and so forth. In the context of the seven seals, each seal is but one color on a canvas. In a painting, the colors have an artistic ordering, but the end result is not the climax of a series but a unity. The impact of a painting is in the total effect of all the colors rather than the ordering of the colors. Instead of a historical sequence, the vision of the opening of the seven seals represents the totality of history.

> ### Seal of Approval
>
> A signet ring was pressed into a dab of wax hardened into a seal on a letter or scroll. A seal served two purposes: First, the wax kept a document closed until a reader opened it; second, the pattern of the imprint was unique to an individual, and thus acted as a signature to identify the owner.

Following the scene of heavenly worship, John the Seer views the opening of the seven seals on the scroll that had been in the hand of God (5:1). Although the seals are opened in heaven, the effects are felt mainly on earth: war, economic difficulties, disease, disaster, and so forth. Events are the various threads that comprise a unity we call "history."

History is the fabric made from the various threads of facts. "In 1492 Columbus sailed the ocean blue," but so did many other sailors. In 1969 Neil Armstrong took "one small step for a man" as his foot touched the moon, but many other people took small steps in 1969. What is to be made of the threads of history? This is the question addressed by John's vision. The focus is not so much on the details of the threads to come, but the vision puts the threads together in way that we see the pattern of the fabric. As much as we want to know the facts, there is a deeper need for the meaning of the facts.

Consider the facts of history that John has experienced in the thirty years prior to the composition of this book. About 60 C.E., a devastating series of earthquakes shook the entire Mediterranean world. In 62 C.E., the invincible Roman legions were soundly thrashed by armies of Parthia (present-day Iran). In 64 C.E., the Christians were blamed for the great fire of Rome and many suffered and died. According to the Roman historians, Christians were arrested and cruelly murdered: dressed in animal skins and given over to wild dogs, nailed to crosses, and even burned alive as "luminaries" at night. In 66–70 C.E., there was a bloody civil war in Judea, culminating in the absolute destruction of Jerusalem and the Temple. In the middle of this civil war, the emperor Nero committed suicide and four Roman generals battled for the imperial throne. In 79 C.E., Mount Vesuvius erupted, burying whole cities and casting a dark cloud of dust over the entire Mediterranean. People thought the world was coming to an end. In 92 C.E., crop failures leading to a famine were crippling the entire Roman empire. With the disruption of food supplies by war and natural disasters, malnutrition made populations ever more susceptible to diseases. And Christians, like their Lord, were liable to suffer at the hands of both imperial and local leadership, to suffer even to death.

> "Through its worship and prayer, the church is intimately linked with the real world, the world of God."—Boring, *Revelation,* Interpretation, 133.

> "The path to the kingdom goes through, not around, the woes of history."—Boring, *Revelation,* Interpretation, 134.

These are some of the facts of the history that John and his congregations were experiencing: war, conflict, disaster, disease, persecution. John's vision depicts the essence of this history. John sees the divine reality that is over, under, and around all that is happening.

54

The First Four Seals (6:1–8)

The first four seals have been called "the four horsemen of the apocalypse." For with each of the first four
seals, there is a vision of a horseman.
John's vision here is a rebirth of imagery
found in Zechariah 1:7–11; 6:1–8.

"I looked, and there was a white
horse! Its rider had a bow; a crown was
given to him, and he came out conquering and to conquer" (6:2). White is the
symbol of victory throughout the book

> **We Shall Overcome**
>
> The verb *nikaō,* meaning "to conquer or
> overcome," is used seventeen times in the
> book of Revelation. In thirteen of those sev-
> enteen times, the term refers unambiguously
> to the victory of Christ and the believer.

of Revelation. A crown is the symbol of rule. The theme of conquering is applied to Christ and to those who follow Christ. Letting the
book of Revelation speak for itself (and not drawing any other references from other places), these three aspects—the color white, the
crown, and the theme of conquering—would point us toward identifying the first horseman with Christ himself.

In chapter 19, where Christ is described in military terms, he is
viewed in this way: "Then I saw heaven opened, and there was a white
horse! Its rider is called Faithful and True, and in righteousness he
judges and makes war" (19:11). The horseman on the white horse
here is clearly identified with Christ.

Though some commentators suggest that the horseman of 6:2 is
a reference to Parthia, they also cannot deny that the image, to a de-
gree, points to Christ as well (Boring, 122–23). If we use the book of
Revelation as the guide to the nature of the symbolism of this first
horseman, it would build a strong argument that the first horseman
is intended to be Christ. That being the case, all else John's vision will
say about the nature of history is grounded at the beginning by
Christ: the one who rode out as conquering and to conquer.

The next horseman, on the red horse, is described in this way:
"And out came another horse, bright red; its rider was permitted to
take peace from the earth, so that people would slaughter one another; and he was given a great sword" (6:4). It takes no great insight
to see that this horseman represents war, the social strife between human beings that leads to killing, maiming, and the destruction of
property. And that horseman still rides. One aspect of the nature of
history is the evil of war. John knew it, and we know it.

The next horseman, on the black horse, is famine. He represents the ecological disasters that strike the earth. And the tragic thing about famine, about ecological disasters, is that the daily necessities are priced out of range of the average worker ("a quart of wheat for a day's wages"), while the luxuries are protected ("do not damage the olive trees and the vineyard"). John knew that famine meant a dearth of necessities for the many, while luxuries abounded for the few. In a world where my dog eats better each day than a third of the children of this planet, this black horse still rides. One aspect of the nature of history is the evil of famine in the midst of luxuries.

The fourth horseman, on the pale-colored horse, is Death (together with his companion Hades). Death comes by "sword, famine, and pestilence, and by the wild animals of the earth" (6:8). The language here is traditional; the experience universal (Boring, 123, notes multiple uses of these images in Jeremiah and Ezekiel). "Sword, famine, and pestilence" still rule. Though many of us avoid the sword and famine, we Americans, in one of the most modern societies of the world, live with cancer rates that are higher per person than in many of the less-developed countries. Death by wild animals may not be frequent, but is high on the fear level: note our fear of sharks, snakes, and large, unkempt dogs. The fourth horseman is at war with our world, and is still a part of us.

The opening of the first four seals gives us what has been called "the four horsemen of the Apocalypse." The first horseman is Christ himself: standing at the beginning of our history of war, famine, and tragic death.

The Fifth Seal (6:9–11)

The opening of the fifth seal does not reveal another horse but rather another tragedy of human history: "When he opened the fifth seal, I saw under the altar the souls of those who had been slaughtered for the word of God and for the testimony they had given" (6:9). One aspect of the nature of history that John knew, and that countless other martyrs have known, is that persecution for the faith can and will happen. John numbers it in his vision; persecution will happen, but he sees more than just tragedy:

> Once again he gives us a profound image with which to reinterpret the meaning of things. The chopping-block of the Roman executioner has become a cosmic altar. Christians who refused to sacrifice to the

image of the emperor are nonetheless Christian priests who sacrifice themselves on the true altar of God. The image used metaphorically by Paul (Rom. 12:1) is filled with stark literalness in John's situation. (Boring, 125)

The cry of the martyrs is "How long will it be before you judge and avenge our blood on the inhabitants of the earth?" (6:10). The question in heaven is the question that also reverberates in the hearts of those on earth, those under the threat of suffering. Although couched in terms of vindication, the vision also emphasizes the connection between earth and heaven. Frederick Faber's hymn "There's a Wideness in God's Mercy" declares: "There is no place where earth's sorrows are more felt than up in heaven."

The call for patience is appropriate for heaven and earth. Those in heaven wait in white robes and in proleptic victory ("proleptic" is wonderful word: it means the representation or assumption of a future event as if it already existed or is already present). Those on earth wait, knowing they are not alone in waiting and that martyrdom is not the final word on their life, should it come to that.

The Sixth Seal (6:12–17)

The fifth seal concerning religious persecution affected a narrow group: those who were faithful in times of great trial. The sixth seal is as broad as can be: here are cosmic-size disasters. The disaster imagery is traditional apocalyptic language (e.g., Mark 13:1–36, Matt. 24:1–43; Luke 22:1–36; Acts 2:14–21; compare Joel 2:30–31). Interestingly enough, the imagery here is more subdued than much of the extrabiblical, apocalyptic material, which glories in the details of cosmic disasters.

> "All in all, these . . . visions produce quite a multimedia show. Just think what John could have produced with modern technology."—C. Freeman Sleeper, *The Victorious Christ,* 48.

No one can escape natural disasters, not even the most powerful people in the world. When the earthquake shakes, rich and poor quiver; when the hurricane blows, strong and weak are buffeted. All are shaken: "the kings of the earth and the magnates and the generals and the rich and the powerful, and everyone, slave and free" (6:15). There is no place to hide. So another aspect of the evil experienced in history is in such natural disasters.

The concluding question of this sixth seal is "Who is able to stand?" (6:17). The sequence is halted here, and there is an interlude (7:1–17) which addresses this question. We will look at this interlude in the next chapter. Those who can stand are those who are sealed by their faith and by their baptism: the church militant and triumphant. Bracketing this interlude now, we move to the opening of the seventh seal.

The Seventh Seal (8:1–5)

After all the momentous seals—war, famine, sickness unto death, religious persecution, natural disasters—the seventh seal is silence in heaven. What is silence for? Silence is for listening. Silence is the

preparatory step to responding: in this case, responding to our prayers. The angel at the altar burns incense in a golden censer and mixes in the prayers of the faithful. Incense has the capacity to fill air space, to penetrate and invade every place. As a pastor who experimented with some frankincense one Epiphany Sunday, I found that a little bit of incense goes a long way! A piece of frankincense, half the size of a dime, when placed on a glowing coal, made a cloud of smoke that rose and wafted up into the choir loft, leaving choir members in a fog. The smell of the incense permeated the sanctuary, balconies, and side transepts, and hung on for several hours. John sees our prayers in this fashion; prayer rises up to the presence of God, not falling short or forgotten, permeating the entire space of heaven.

"The smoke of the incense rose before God."

The confidence of the vision is that prayer works. The angel fills the censer with fire from the altar and casts it down upon the earth. There will be vindication for those who are under the same altar, those who pray "How long?" There will be security for those who are in the struggle, as the interlude between the sixth and seventh seals indicates (which we will address in the next unit):

John's revelation lets the worshiping church see its prayer from the heavenward side. . . . The prayers are "heard"; they have an effect. The effect is not merely the subjective release in the worshiper; the prayers of the saints on earth cause things to happen on the earth (8:4–5; cf. 9:13–14). The saints' prayers do not result in deliverance from historical troubles but the deliverance of the world and history by the eschatological appearance of God's kingdom. (Boring, 133)

The silence of the seventh seal represents the confidence that God hears. For John the Seer, in the "spirit on the Lord's day" (1:10; compare 4:2); his own trials and the trials of his congregations are swept up into the very presence of God.

The first seal and the last occupy the place of preeminence: Christ, the conqueror who conquers, and prayers that make it to the presence of God. In between is the stuff of history. Within the bounds set by Christ and prayer, the evil of history is to be faced. We can number the evils of history: war, famine, death, persecution, and disaster. These evils are part of the nature of history: no surprises here. But they are only a portion of the vision. To treat them alone would be like constructing a rainbow of only one color. What sets the evils of history in perspective is Christ at the beginning and prayer at the end. Those who are sealed by God (7:1–17), sealed in baptism, are able to stand in this chaos, as we will see in the next chapter.

Want to Know More?

About incense? See J. G. Davies, ed., *The New Westminster Dictionary of Liturgy and Worship* (Philadelphia: Westminster Press, 1986), 265–66.

About silence? See E. Glenn Hinson, *Spirituality in Ecumenical Perspective* (Louisville, Ky.: Westminster John Knox Press, 1993), 34–37.

About the End Times? See William Barclay, *At the Last Trumpet: Jesus Christ and the End of Time* (Louisville, Ky.: Westminster John Knox Press, 1998); for a thorough discussion of the philosophical implications, see Ulrich H. J. Körtner, *The End of the World: A Theological Interpretation* (Louisville, Ky.: Westminster John Knox Press, 1995).

Eugene Peterson, in teaching this section of Revelation in a church Bible study, tells of a woman stopping him and asking if she could tell her story. Years previously, she told him and the group, she had had a nervous breakdown. Her whole life was chaos; nothing fit together. She was unglued, "unsealed" as it were.

She went to a counselor and was guided to name the chaos, detail by detail. None of the chaos became any less horrible or palatable as she did this. But something else happened; she discovered things in her life that had been obscured by this overbearing lump of evil. She had some relationships that were delightful; there was music that she could enjoy, sights that caused her to pause. Her own body was working, most of it fairly well. As she connected with faith and trust in God, she began to feel that there was more than the chaos of life. None of the evil was abolished or taken away. But the proportions had shifted, the perspective transformed. Nothing in her life had changed; everything in her life was changed. The unsealing chaos of history was ringed by a larger circle: that Christ was at the beginning and prayer was at the end (Peterson, 85–86).

? Questions for Reflection

1. Sometimes we seal up treasures from a particular time period for opening at a point in the future—in a time capsule. Usually these are items that will reveal the thoughts and feelings of that time period. What are the thoughts and feelings revealed in the seven seals of these chapters? As with previous units, do these images conjure up a message of hope or doom? Why?

2. The problems and struggles of history continue to persist: war, famine, death, persecution, and disaster. Are there solutions to these problems? If so, why haven't the solutions been enacted? If not, how does the message of Revelation speak to these problems?

3. This unit affirmed a verse from an old hymn, "There is no place where earth's sorrows are more felt than up in heaven." What do you think this verse means? What other hymns does this call to mind for you?

4. At the breaking of the seventh seal, there is silence (8:1). What is the purpose of silence? Where are the moments of silence in your life? Are there benefits to silence? Why or why not?

Revelation 7:1–17   **7**

The Church Triumphant

One of the great dramatic techniques is suspense. The movie direc-
tor Alfred Hitchcock was a master of this technique in movies as well
as in person. There is a story told of a practical joke pulled by Hitchcock on unsuspecting people in hotel elevators. He would board an
elevator with a friend and immediately begin telling the friend of an
episode that took place the prior evening at home. Following standard elevator decorum, the other passengers simply looked straight
ahead at the door, pretending not to listen but enjoying the opportunity to overhear.

It seemed, Hitchcock would say, that after he climbed into his bed,
he heard furtive scratching at his door. After listening for a time, hoping the sound would go away, he took the baseball bat that he kept
under his bed and moved to the door. With bat in hand he slowly began to turn the knob of the door. In the telling of the story, Hitchcock would time this part of the story to when the elevator doors
opened for the floor to which he was going. Then he would walk out
of the elevator with his companion, leaving the other passengers behind. Then he would say, "And as I eased open the door, I saw . . ."
This "I saw" was timed with the closing of the elevator doors, so that
those remaining in the elevator, who had been overhearing the story,
were left with nothing more. They were left in suspense.

John the Seer uses the dramatic technique of suspense in his vision
of the opening of the seven seals; between the sixth and the seventh
seal, there is an intervening vision. The literary result is suspense, with
the added dimension of highlighting this intervening vision. We are
invited to lean forward to hear about the culminating seventh seal,
but our attention is directed toward another vital matter: the nature

and composition of the people of God. The surprising work of God is evident:

> Instead of seeing the expected End, what we see is the church. This is literary craftsmanship, but more than that—it is a reflection of the experience of first-century Christianity. They looked for the End and what came was the church, not as a substitute for the act of God but itself a dimension of God's saving activity. (Boring, 127)

The interlude vision in 7:1–17 addresses the final question of the sixth seal: "Who can stand?" The sixth seal, with cosmic shaking of the world, engulfs everyone. This interlude shows the secure reality of the people of God in the chaos of history, particularly as evidenced by the second through the sixth seals.

Baptism as Seal

After establishing the pause in the chaos of history—the four angels holding back the winds (7:1–2)—the vision moves quickly to answer the question, "Who can stand?" John sees that some have been sealed (7:3). The image of sealing is multivalent. First, in the context of unsealing seven seals, there is a sealing going on as well. Second, typical of John's vision, this sealing on the forehead is not a new image but rather a reinterpretation of an Old Testament vision: Ezekiel 9:1–11. Those so marked in Ezekiel's vision live through the tragedy of being conquered. Likewise, those sealed in John's vision live through, but are not exempted from, the trying times that are coming: the devastating wind (7:1–3) and the demonic locusts (9:3–4). Third, this sealing mark contrasts the "mark of the beast" on the forehead and hand (13:16–17; 14:9). The "beast" is a primary symbol for the persecuting power of Rome. (For more on this, see the following unit.) Eugene Boring (129) aptly notes: "Evil has no independent existence; its supposed power is only a counterfeit of the real power of the Lamb." Imitation, it is said, is the sincerest form of flattery. The "mark of the beast" is a pale imitation of the sealing of the people of God.

> "The 'seal' of God does not mark believers for protection against evil, but only from being defeated by it."—González and González, *Revelation*, Westminster Bible Companion, 57.

One further overtone to this sealing language connects to baptism:

> Incorporation into the body of Christ by baptism (I Cor. 12:13) was sometimes pictured in Pauline churches as the seal which stamped the new Christian as belonging to God (II Cor. 1:22; Eph. 1:13; 4:30). In the midst of the Roman threat baptism comes to have a new meaning: those who bear the mark of God are kept through (not from!) the coming great ordeal, whatever the beastly powers of evil may be able to do to them. (Boring, 129)

Baptism is not a talisman to ward off evil, but it does set us apart as belonging to God. When the world is becoming unsealed, baptism seals us.

The Poetry of the Numbers

The nature and character of those who are sealed comes in two succeeding visions—actually a "hearing" and then a "seeing." The Seer first hears a very specific number: 144,000 drawn from the twelve tribes of Israel. Then, typical of the experience of "hearing something," the Seer turns toward the sound and sees. The second vision is of the vast multitude that "no one can number." The visions are of the same reality: the people of God. Contrary to a chronological reading (e.g., the first vision: faithful Jews; the second vision: the Gentile church), the two visions are like a rhyme.

In the poetry with which we are perhaps most familiar, meaning is highlighted and emphasized by using words that have similar sounds, but different meanings: "I think that I shall never see a poem lovely as a tree"—Joyce Kilmer; "Humpty Dumpty sat on a wall. Humpty Dumpty had a great fall"—Mother Goose. Rhyming is used for emphasis.

In the poetry of the Old Testament, the Hebrew poets did not rhyme sounds but rather "rhymed" meanings. That is, they would say the same thing twice in different ways: not a rhyme of sound as in "rhyme, time" but rather a rhyme of meaning: "verse, stanza." This technique of rhyming meanings is seen throughout the Psalms and the prophets. Isaiah says, "Though your sins are like scarlet, they shall be like snow; though they are red like crimson, they shall become like wool (Isa. 1:18). Psalm 127:1 declares, "Unless the LORD builds the house, those who build it labor in vain. Unless the LORD guards the city, the guard keeps watch in vain."

John hears a number (Rev. 7:4–8) on earth; he sees a number in heaven (7:9–10). If you miss the rhyme between the two visions, you will think that two different groups are being talked about. But the writer has in mind the same group, viewed from different perspectives. The earthly hearing is very specific: the restored Israel in a "square number" of 144,000, the twelve tribes of twelve thousand. The people of God are a "perfect" number but they are a limited number. The heavenly seeing has no such limits of clan or number: "a great multitude that no one could count, from every nation, from all tribes and peoples and languages" (7:9).

Want to Know More?

About the 144,000? See William Barclay, *The Book of Revelation*, vol. 2, Daily Study Bible (Philadelphia: Westminster Press, 1976), 24–27.

About Hebrew poetry? See Bruce M. Metzger and Ronald E. Murphy, "Characteristics of Hebrew Poetry," in *The New Oxford Annotated Bible* (NRSV) (New York: Oxford University Press, 1991), 392–97.

The 144,000

The first vision that he hears is that the people of God are 144,000 strong, all from the twelve tribes of Israel. Note that 144,000 is a square number—12 times 12 equals 144 (then multiplied by one thousand). In John's day, there was no Arabic number system. Numbers were visualized in terms of a series of dots. One hundred forty-four dots (each dot=thousand) would form a square, a perfect sort of number.

This square-shaped body of the sealed are from the twelve tribes of Israel. Already we have seen that Israel is not the Jews but the church (e.g., Rev. 3:9, those in the synagogue who "say that they are Jews and are not"). The church on earth is the New Israel: chosen, perfectly shaped, exclusively defined, and limited. This earthly vision that John hears is contrasted to the rhyming vision, the vision that he turns and sees.

"The church in this picture is not only big, it is complete. The number 144,000 is a complete, fulfilled number."—Boring, *Revelation*, Interpretation, 130.

John turns and sees an enormous crowd that cannot be numbered. In contrast to the perfect shape of a square, this vision is of a great blob of people. Instead of being numbered only from the tribes of Israel, it is completely inclusive: "from every nation, from all tribes and peoples and languages" (7:9). And instead of a set number, this vision of the people of God is of a mass that is uncountable.

The limited number—144,000—are sealed for the coming ordeal. The term "thousand" is used in the Old Testament as a division of the military. The 144 "thousands" are arrayed for war; the battle is not done on this earth, as the limited church fights the good fight. The second vision shifts the scene to heaven, where the great ordeal is done and there is no limit to those who have conquered, those who wear the white robe and wave the palm branch. The two images give contrasting views of the church: limited and battling; unlimited and victorious.

> "John resists the temptation to think smugly of only the 'faithful few' who are genuine Christians."—Boring, *Revelation*, Interpretation, 130.

Rhyming visions are paired here, each with its emphasis. Here is that biblical tension between election and universal inclusion, between a set number of God's people and complete freedom as to who will be a part of the God's people, between the struggle and the victory, between the Church Militant and the Church Triumphant. Both are true and stand in tension in the now.

A Future Now

The heavenly vision is not put in terms of the future. The reality of the victorious multitude that no one can number is declared in the present tense of the Seer: "After this I looked, and there was a great multitude . . ." (7:9). For those who remain in the struggle, it is the future and *what will be*. For John the Seer, the vision is the present and *what is now*. The good news of the second vision is that the future determines and creates the present: those who are sealed will be victorious in Christ.

The concluding hymnic ascription to this vision is the sheltering and shepherding that takes place in the presence of God (7:15–17). In yet another clue that the book of Revelation is not to be read in a chronological sequence, this final declaration has nearly all the elements of the final, climactic vision beginning at 21:1—light, shelter, worship, no hunger, no thirst, no tears, eternity. There is no need for anything else to be said or seen, and yet much more will come after this vision. In some ways, the book of Revelation is like the action of a student pilot practicing touching down on a landing strip: the plane touches down, bounces back into the sky, circles the landing area, touches down again, and the cycle is repeated. In other words, instead of a linear development from one point to the next, the book develops as a spiral around the reality of the victorious Lamb upon the throne.

The rendering of the tense of the verbs in this final hymnic ascription may obscure the solid, secure landing area. Balmer Kelly questions the typical translation of these in the future tense:

> Many times the future tense is the mode of stating absolute fact and is correctly rendered by the English emphatic present. So in the present passage it makes good sense to translate the verbs of the hymn at the end in this fashion. God *does* dwell with them; they *do not* hunger; God *does* wipe away all tears. (Kelly, 294)

Instead of a "now" and "not yet," the Seer lays out the continuity, connection, and unity of the communion of the saints. The limited and fixed Church Militant—the 144,000—holds on just on the periphery of the inclusive and unlimited Church Triumphant—the number that no one can number.

"And he will guide them to springs of life" (Rev. 7:17).

Anticipating the vision of the new Jerusalem in Revelation 21, this interlude (7:1–17) between the sixth and seventh seals answers the question of "who can stand" in the chaos of history. The suspense in awaiting the opening of the final seal diminishes in importance and impact. The destiny of the Church Militant and Triumphant is assured. Indeed, looking beyond the seventh seal, further woes will be brought out in the series of seven trumpets and seven bowls, which are to follow. However, there is no historical or chronological progression intended or implied, as if first one thing must happen and then another. Like the ongoing heavenly worship that surrounds and undergirds the church's worship (Revelation 4–5), the chaos of history is encompassed by the reality of the security of the people of God. In this interlude, the Seer proclaims the "heavenly present," which is real and now. Although it is the future for those who still struggle on this earth, it is the future that determines this present: those who can stand are those who have conquered with the Lamb, who have been washed in the blood, who have been sealed by their baptism.

William Walsham How put this faith into poetic form in the hymn, "For All the Saints":

> And when the fight is fierce, the warfare long,
> Steals on the ear the distant triumph song,
> And hearts are brave again, and arms are strong.
> Alleluia! Alleluia!

In the midst of the chaotic and destructive forces that shake this world, the future of the people of God is not in suspense: they come through the great ordeal.

> "The point is clear. Christian faithfulness, while a human act, is enabled by divine grace."—Charles H. Talbert, *The Apocalypse*, 37.

? Questions for Reflection:

1. This unit notes the strong baptismal imagery of this passage. Why are individuals baptized? Why are there different understandings of baptism across Christian traditions? What is the importance of baptism in this passage?
2. The number of the church is described as a perfect number. What does the term "perfect" mean? Knowing that every church is composed of ordinary humans, frailties and all, how can the term "perfect" be used to describe the church?
3. Verses 9–10 remind us of the scene in the Gospels of Jesus' entrance into Jerusalem (compare Matt. 21:8–9). Compare these two scenes. The word "hosanna" means "Lord, save us." How does this bit of information change your understanding of each passage?
4. This unit suggests that some of the realities of the triumphant church can be experienced now, that God *does* dwell with us and *does* wipe away tears. How does one reconcile this glorious vision with our contemporary context? How is God's dwelling with us known? What does it mean to suggest that God wipes away our tears?

8 Revelation 13:1-18

A Beastly Power

Since the proverbial declaration is that "confession is good for the soul," I confess that my Social Security number ends with the numbers "666." The reactions of people when I supply my Social Security number for identification purposes are often quite amusing. One even advised me that I ought to get that number changed. After all, 666 is the mark of the beast!

Revelation 13:1-18, with its concluding reference to the "mark of the beast" (13:17-18), has captivated imagination and speculation for centuries. Imagination is a key word here, because God works in the imaginative and poetic vision of John the Seer. However, instead of looking for the mark of the beast in our own situation, we will continue to orient that imagination to the pastoral situation of first-century Christians. In other words, what would the mark of the beast mean to John's hearers? Before addressing this mark, we first must identify the beast. And, in fact, there are two beasts: the beast from the sea and the beast from the land. Our approach to the fantastic vision of Revelation 13 is to ask: What would this beast from the sea and the beast from the land mean to John's congregations?

> "[Revelation 12–13] pulls away the curtain that hides the transcendent world from ordinary sight and offers a behind-the-scenes view of the powers of evil at work in the present."—Boring, *Revelation*, Interpretation, 150.

The Beast from the Sea (13:1-10)

The beast from the sea is incited by the dragon to persecute the people of God. The previous chapter (Revelation 12) details the work of the dragon in its failure at war with God and with Christ. So the dragon turns his evil on those who follow Christ—the "saints" (which is another word for Christians, and not a reference to extraordinary Christians). The dragon (Satan or the devil) is seen as the force behind the beast from the sea. And for John it is clear that beast is an embodiment of the Roman Empire.

This identification with the Roman Empire is verified in several ways. First, the description of the sea beast (ten horns, leopard, bear, etc.) is an adaptation of a vision in the book of Daniel (Dan. 7:1ff.) where four beasts come out of the sea. In the book of Daniel each of the four beasts is identified specifically with an empire that wars against the saints of God. The sea beast of Revelation 13 is a conglomeration of the four beasts of Daniel 7. Using the interpretive direction set by Daniel, the sea beast is the ultimate beastly kingdom that is warring on the saints. The most likely candidate at the end of the first century is thus the Roman Empire.

The identification of this beastly kingdom with the Roman Empire receives further confirmation in Revelation 17, where it is identified with the "harlot" city that is built on seven hills (Rev. 17:9, compare 17:18). Even today it is proverbial to speak of Rome as "the city built on seven hills," connected with the story of the founding of Rome by Romulus (Mounce, 315–16). So the book of Revelation itself gives a very specific clue as to the identity of the beast.

Finally, the characteristics of the sea beast fit the experience of the Roman Empire by Christians in Asia Minor at the turn of the first century.

Coins bore the emperor's image and titles.

1. *"From the sea."* Roman armies, governors, and other representatives of the empire came to Asia Minor by sea. Each of the cities mentioned in the seven letters had a long history of independence and autonomy, which had been ceded to Rome.

2. *Mouth uttering blasphemies against God.* Beginning with Augustus Caesar (the Roman ruler at the time of Jesus' birth) some one hundred years before the writing of the book of Revelation,

every Roman ruler took on more and more titles that were divine. By the time of the writing of the book of Revelation, the Roman ruler Domitian was to be addressed as "Lord and God." And the common people knew these titles because the very coins that they used bore a likeness of the Roman ruler and one or more of his divine titles. In our context, it would be like altering pennies, nickels, and quarters from "In God we trust" to "Lincoln is God," "Jefferson is Lord," and "Washington is God." In the day-to-day exchange of coins, the expressions of blasphemy would pass from hand to hand.

3. *Authority over the world.* The Roman Empire stretched across most of the "known world" for the first-century people of Asia Minor. The Roman name for the Mediterranean Sea was *Mare Nostrum:* "Our Sea." They had good reason for this name as their rule extended from England, to Europe, to Northern Africa, to the Middle East.

4. *War on the saints.* The traditional view of the setting of the book of Revelation is that John is writing in a time when the Roman Empire is making a concerted and systematic effort to destroy the church. The actions of Emperor Nero some thirty years prior to the writing of the book (to be treated further below) horrified both Christians and pagan Roman historians. In the earliest histories of the church (second to fourth centuries), there is a clear belief that there was widespread and official persecution in John's day. John's residence on Patmos appears to be an official banishment from his home in Asia Minor (see 1:9). Three of the seven letters to the churches indicate that some persecution has taken place: at Ephesus (2:2–3); Pergamum (2:13), and Philadelphia (3:8–10). There is about to be suffering and imprisonment in Smyrna (2:10), and there is a warning to those in Philadelphia of an "hour of trial that is coming on the whole world" (3:10). In the opening of the fifth seal (6:10), we saw those who were martyred for their faith. In 17:6, Rome is the harlot Babylon, drunk with the blood of the martyrs. Revelation gives many indications of the current and impending persecution of Christians, though recent scholarship has questioned how widespread the persecution may have been in John's day. (Boring, 13–18, reviews the evidences for official state persecution.)

5. *"One of its heads seemed to have received a death-blow, but its mortal wound had been healed" (13:3).* Nero instigated a partic-

ularly cruel and savage persecution of Christians to avert suspicions that he was responsible for a tragic fire in Rome in 64 C.E. He took his own life in 68, but rumors persisted that he was still alive. Indeed, several pretenders arose claiming to be Nero. By the end of the first century there was the belief that he would rise from the dead and seize power. Nero fits the description of a head that has received a death-blow but who lives through the mortal wound.

Our Response to Government

The beast from the sea is the Roman Empire. However, it is somewhat misleading simply to say the beast is Rome. Rome was in some sense the latest embodiment of the beastly kingdoms (see Daniel 7:1ff.). This beast for us as present-day readers is broader than the Roman Empire. The beast is the misuse of government, where it falls under the power of the dragon. It is important to note that it is the misuse of government that is beastly, not the action of governing.

The Bible clearly recognizes the human need for government. In fact, government, says Paul in Romans 13, is an instrument of God. Our faithful duty is to be good citizens, according to Paul. But government's greatest temptation is to become like the beast: that is, to misuse violence to bring about an overreaching obedience and loyalty, to use its authority to force obedience.

Beastly governments range across history from long ago to recent times: the murderous rule of Pol Pot in Cambodia, the violent and deadly subjection of the students in Tiananmen Square in Beijing, the crimes of Pinochet in Chile, and so forth. The state's use of overt violence to force loyalty continues. The temptation of governing is to impose, by punishment or by violence, obedience beyond its bounds.

> "The whole passage calls responsible interpreters of the Bible not to 'decoding' a 'puzzle' but to alertness in discerning the nature and consequences of one's commitments."—Boring, *Revelation*, Interpretation, 164.

The writer of the book of Revelation sets out the vision of the beast who comes from the sea—the Roman Empire was its latest embodiment—and the beast is still with us. Other parts of the New Testament, particularly Romans 13, express the view that government is one of the defenses established by God to contain the powers of evil in society. Revelation 13 sees the depraved and fallen side of government. It is the beast that demands loyalty and obedience that goes only to God and to God's agenda for the world: peace and justice. (A convenient way to remember these two conceptions of government is that they are found in chapter 13 of the two New Testament books that start with "R": Romans and Revelation.)

So what does one do before the beast? John gives this counsel: "Let anyone who has an ear listen: If you are to be taken captive, into captivity you go; if you kill with the sword, with the sword you must be killed. Here is a call for the endurance and faith of the saints" (13:9–10). In this pastoral counsel, there is a bit of fatalism; if any are to be taken captive, to captivity they go. But there is more; John discourages adopting the methods of the beast.

When we live in a world of violence long enough, it is easy to adopt violent means ourselves, especially when we know that our cause is righteous and the opposition is evil.

> Religious faith, especially when zealous, is no stranger to the exercise of violent force . . . [And so John warns his readers] not to defect into violence. Had not Jesus, in as violent a scene as any of us will find ourselves, said, "Put your sword back into its place; for all who live by the sword will perish by the sword"? (Matt. 26:52). Killing the opposition is the sea beast's way of solving its problems. It is not ours. (Peterson, 125)

Or is it our way? We stand in the tradition of armed revolution against an established government, the American Revolution. John Witherspoon, a Presbyterian minister, signed the Declaration of Independence. Rebellion was preached from many a pulpit. The institutionalized violence on both economic and civil freedoms imposed by the British on their colonies was met with overt violence: rebellion.

So violence in the name of religion is no stranger to our history. One way the beast has been met is with counter violence. But to take such action is to adopt the means of the beast. John, echoing Jesus, proclaims that violent means only tarnish and destroy the best of our intentions.

John's pastoral counsel is endurance and faith. In some sense, John expresses a form of Christian pacifism. But not dumb passivity or unthought-out giving up! John clings to the meaning of the victory found in the cross; Christ's followers are called upon to embrace sacrifice and even death because these are the most aggressive forces to be used in the raging battle between God and the devil.

One of the most horrifying and yet moving scenes in the movie *Ghandi* takes place when Ghandi organizes a strike against a British electric utility. The strikers block the entrance to the plant so trucks cannot get in. They stand in rows of four and do not disperse when ordered to do so. The British guards batter the front four strikers with clubs to clear the way, but then four more protestors step forward to be battered in the same fashion. Over and over again, the scene is repeated. After a while the guards are panting and exhausted from administering the beatings, but still more protestors step forward, without raising a hand in their defense. It was an aggressive sort of endurance that they demonstrated—an endurance that wears out those who would beat them.

John's view of how to deal with the beast is not the only biblical view but it is one that must be heard and attended to. He calls not for rebellion or surrender, but endurance and faith. Compared to the use of force it is certainly the more Christlike response, more in line with Jesus' own facing of the cross with endurance and faith. John's confidence is that the beast loses each time he strikes a Christian down. The victory belongs to the Lamb and to those who follow the Lamb.

The beast from the sea is not alone, however, in the war against the saints. There is also the beast from the land.

The Beast from the Land (13:11–18)

The "beast from the land" serves the beast from the sea. Elsewhere, this beast is called the "false prophet" (16:13; 19:20; 20:10). The land beast is the representative of the sea beast, promoting and demanding "faithfulness" to the sea beast. Coming from the earth is, as it were, this beast is native and indigenous. But this beast from the land is intimately connected to the sea beast, enforcing loyalty and devotion.

So here is what we are looking for: a first-century entity that would strike the early Christians as beastly, that was homegrown or "of the land," and tied intimately to the Roman Empire, the beast from the sea. In fact, its function is to promote worship of that beast from the sea, the Roman Empire. Not to worship the beast from the sea brings about the possibility of capital punishment. Not to worship the beast means economic sanctions: one may not buy or sell. Was there anything like that in the life of the Christians to whom John was a pastor?

Starting almost two hundred years before Christ, the Roman Empire was accorded such great respect and awe that it bordered on religious belief in the Mediterranean world. There were occasions where a king, at his death, would will his entire kingdom to the Roman Empire, knowing that it would be the best for his people. At first, people spoke of the spirit of Rome: the goddess Roma. Temples were erected in the Mediterranean world to her. She brought peace, law and order, commerce, good roads, a judicial system. The spirit of Roma was gladly endorsed and accepted.

But then a shift gradually occurred. Instead of focusing on the spirit of Roma, the religious fervor began to center on the emperor himself. It began with the emperor Augustus, the emperor at the time of Jesus' birth. People began to give him divine names. He generally played down such titles and would not let the people of Rome use such titles for him, but if the uneducated masses out in the far reaches of the empire wanted to do so, he reluctantly accepted such tribute as being politically expedient.

But with each emperor after Augustus, the divine titles became more and more prolific. The popularity of emperor worship grew. And by and large, each emperor was less inclined to distance himself from such titles. Such titles had great ego appeal; it is not everyone who gets hailed as a god. But the titles also had great political power. After all, what better uniting force to this empire that stretched from Egypt to England than a common religion?

Divine Right

The idea that the king or emperor rules by divine consent or ancestry is ancient (even pre-Roman). Some emperors and monarchs spin out elaborate apologetics and genealogies to show their divine appointment (and, for some, even that they are descendants of Caesar), and thus their right to rule. For an overview of the development of divine titles for Roman rulers, see Boring, *Revelation*, Interpretation, 18–21.

What began as a popular movement became organized into a regular religion; worship of the emperor, worship of Caesar. It was not an exclusive religion; one could worship other gods as well. In some ways, it was an expression of political loyalty more than anything else.

The area where emperor worship was most developed and most fervently followed was in the area of present-day Turkey, the location of the churches to which John was writing. The cities of Asia competed for the honor of building temples for the worship of Rome and of Caesar. Local councils, a native groups of priests, oversaw the emperor worship. They were not from Rome; they were natives of the land, who had the authority of Rome behind them as they led the worship of the emperor.

The pressure to participate in emperor worship was strong. Although we do not know all the details, we can surmise what was required of Christians.

> According to a tradition that probably represents the actual situation, they were required to make the two-word acknowledgment of Roman sovereignty, "*Kurios Kaisaros*" ("Caesar is Lord"), an exact counterpart to the basic Christian confession "Jesus is Lord" (cf. Rom. 10:9; I Cor. 12:3). In addition, they were required to curse Christ. We have documentation that those in later periods who complied were given a certificate exempting them from persecution. Although we have no specific evidence, it is likely that even in John's day those who complied were given some kind of certification. . . . Those who did not comply could be tortured or executed. (Boring, 18)

The beast from the land that threatened first-century Christians was this organization of emperor worship. Every Christian who would not say "Caesar is Lord and God" could potentially became an outlaw. Without the mark of the beast—the certificate showing that indeed you had pledged allegiance to Caesar as God—persecution and arrest could take place, though it did not always happen. But it hung over their heads. Who was Lord? Christ or Caesar?

The organization and propagation of emperor worship became a beastly presence to Christians. In the hands of the priests of emperor worship rested the livelihood of Christians who could not on the basis of their faith say that Caesar was Lord. The land beast was the false prophet of the sea beast.

The Mark of the Beast (13:18)

In the year 2015, the world financial community comes up with a new credit card system. A miniature computer chip, smaller than the point of needle, will be injected into a person's hand. Then, instead of writing a check or using a credit card to make a purchase, a person will simply move his hand underneath a scanner and the purchase will be recorded. No need for cash; no need for checks; no need for credit cards. Each person will be able to buy and sell, with the wave of the hand. And just suppose that the company that produces and installs these microchips has an address of 666 Main Street. Have people just received the mark of the beast that will allow them "to buy and sell" as John describes it in the thirteenth chapter of Revelation? We need to say a clear "No!" But people have been making up such scenarios for years to explain the beastly mark in the book of Revelation.

Again, our task is to consider this mark and this number in the context of the first century. In this case, the reference to the beast is a reference to the dominant beast, that is, the beast from the sea. It is the mark of the sea beast, the Roman Empire (the beast from the land is the prophet for this beast). If we are to find an explanation of it, we are to look toward the Roman Empire.

> "A valuable dimension of this imagery is that it pictures the vastness of the reservoir of evil by which we are threatened and from which we cannot deliver ourselves. 'Cosmic' is not too big a word; 'dragon' is not too bizarre an image."—Boring, *Revelation*, Interpretation, 167.

John says: "Let anyone with understanding calculate the number of the beast, for it is the number of a person. Its number is six hundred sixty-six" (13:18). Oh, the debate and time spent on this number! But John, the writer, thinks that the reader will know what it means.

Within a hundred years after the book of Revelation was written, one of the most learned Christians of the day, named Irenaeus, was not sure what it meant (so we should not be too hard on ourselves for having difficulty with this number). In fact, there is even a problem as to whether the six hundred sixty-six is the original number that the writer of Revelation wrote. Some of the most ancient manuscripts of Revelation have 616 instead of 666. (This alternative reading is footnoted in such translations as the RSV and NRSV.) Scholars who consider the various manuscripts of the Bible and try to evaluate what is the most original reading are reasonably sure that 666 is the proper reading, but early on there are manuscripts that read 616.

This number, 666 or 616, is the number of a human who is connected to the beast from the sea, the Roman Empire. How could a human being have a number? Quite easily. This was the day before our Arabic number system. There were no specific number symbols in Greek, Hebrew, or Latin. For example, what we call "Roman numerals" are simply letters of the Latin alphabet. Each society had an agreed-upon code for

Want to Know More?

About Daniel 7? See W. Sibley Towner, *Daniel*, Interpretation (Atlanta: John Knox Press, 1984), 91–115.

About Nero? See William Barclay, *The Revelation of John*, Vol. 2, Daily Study Bible, 88–92; see also George Arthur Buttrick, ed., *The Interpreter's Dictionary of the Bible*, vol. K–Q (Nashville: Abingdon Press, 1962), 537–39.

About the view of government in Romans? See Art Ross and Martha Stevenson, *Romans*, Interpretation Bible Studies (Louisville, Ky.: Geneva Press, 1999), Unit 9.

translating a letter into a specific number. Thus any combination of letters could be added up. Examples of number-plays on a person's name abound. One of the most amusing examples was found on some graffiti on a wall in Pompei (yes, people wrote on walls in those days, too). It reads: "I love the girl whose number is phi mu epsilon (584)." Some girl could add up the letter-numbers in her name and find out if she was the one. In an early Christian writing much like the book of Revelation, Jesus is spoken of as 888 because the addition of the letters of "Jesus" equals 888 (*Sibylline Oracles* 1.324ff.).

The number of a person is likely a name. The problem is, of course, any number of combinations of letters could give 666 (or 616). There are a multitude of combinations of letters that add up to 666 (or 616).

However, the Latin spelling of "Caesar Nero" can be written in Hebrew letters in two ways: the most expected way yields 666 (the alternative way yields 616). Maybe that scribal error of 616 was not so much an error as it was a correction by someone who knew what John was saying. It easy to imagine a scribe, who knows that the number of the beast is the sum of Caesar Nero, wanting to correct John's document. "Wouldn't want John to be known as a person who couldn't add, would we now?" could have been the thought. In other words, this explanation explains both the original reading and the scribal variation.

The interpretation of the beast's number as 666 pointing to Nero has much to warrant it. Nero had been dead for thirty years at the time of the writing of the book of Revelation, but the shadow of his life was still great. This Caesar Nero had begun the state persecution of Christians. Under his hand Paul and Peter were probably martyred. Caesar Nero, according to Roman historians, invented cruel and inhuman ways to kill Christians. The same Caesar Nero, although dead, was expected to come again. In fact, two imposters claiming to be Nero arose in the years after his death and attracted great followings. Nero, or the ghost of Nero, was not dead. His beastly shadow still loomed large. As John saw the onslaught of state-supported or state-blessed persecution, the spirit of Emperor Nero could be seen to be alive.

> **On Your Mark**
>
> On the many possibilities of what might be meant by the mark of the beast, see Boring, pages 161–64. In addition, the number 666 might be understood more symbolically. If the number 7 is a divine number, 777 might represent the holy Trinity with 666 being the flawed imitation of good by evil—an evil trinity comprised by Satan, the sea beast, and the land beast.

What is the human number of the beast? It is 666; it is Caesar Nero and every ruler since who was like him. In the face of all the attempts to identify the number 666 with the pope, Napoleon Bonaparte, Adolf Hitler, a new computerized financial scheme, and so forth, we find an explanation that would make sense to a first-century reader. Etched on the Christian memory was the villainous rule of Nero, whose spirit was on the rise again.

The beastly requirement of Christians in Asia was popular religion. It was not originated by the Romans but rather accepted by them. Such religion marked one's participation in the social good, much as saying the pledge of allegiance or singing the National Anthem is at sporting events. To envision in a very shallow way the stigma that led to persecution, consider the person who attends the local Rotary Club and does not stand for the pledge of allegiance. Consider the affront that many of us feel when athletes (in living color on our television screen) remain seated, chatting and laughing during the National Anthem.

> "All propaganda that entices humanity to idolize human empire is an expression of this beastly power that wants to appear Lamb-like."—Boring, *Revelation,* Interpretation, 157.

John's pastoral word to his readers is this: popular religion must always be met with discernment and wisdom. Before the false claims of popular religion, the Christian is to have understanding. Don't be fooled into saying Caesar is God, even if you do not mean it, for you are tying yourself to the beast. Don't be fooled by saying it doesn't matter what I believe, as long as I am sincere (that's popular religion). Don't be tempted to have no religion at all (that's popular religion). Don't be hoodwinked by New Agers, televangelists, or even Presbyterian preachers: be wise, be discerning, be observant.

? Questions for Reflection

1. Government sure isn't painted attractively in this chapter. What is the proper response to governing powers? How does one determine whether government should be defended or opposed?

2. One of the recurrent themes of the book of Revelation is the call to perseverance. The call returns here at 13:10. What does it mean to persevere? Against what are the readers of Revelation to perse-

vere? In the face of those challenges, what would encourage you to persevere?

3. Revelation 13:8 offers an interesting translation variant. The NRSV reads, " . . . everyone whose name has not been written from the foundation of the world in the book of life of the Lamb that was slaughtered," while other translations place the phrase to read " . . . everyone whose name has not been written in the book of life of the Lamb that was slaughtered from the foundation of the world." How does the placement of the phrase change the meaning of the verse?

4. There are many "marks" in our lives, indicators of groups to which we belong or ideas that we affirm. What are the marks that define you? Why do you bear those marks?

A Thousand Years

Millennium fever! By the time you read this book, you will probably have had your fill of conversation about the new millennium. The biblical roots of this word are found in this section of the book of Revelation and there has been much ink spread on paper and much wringing of hands concerning a very small part of the book of Revelation. Much more vital to John the Seer is the status of congregational life (Rev. 2–3), worship in heaven (Rev. 4–5), the general visions of woes of history in the seven seals (Rev. 6 and 8:1–6), the seven trumpets (8:7–21 and 11:15–19), the seven bowls of wrath (Rev. 16), the future recompense of the harlot city, Rome (Revelation 17–18), and even the final vision of the new Jerusalem (Rev. 21:1–22:5). John's millennial expectation is a small concern in the overall scheme of Revelation. However, given the popular interest and concern about what the Bible says about "the millennium," our task is to examine this section.

"... and locked it for a thousand years."

Seven Visions

Revelation 20:1–15 is part of a sequence of seven visions (no surprise about the number). In this case, instead of marking the seven with seals, trumpets, or bowls, the seven visions are marked by the phrase "Then I saw" (see 19:11, 17, 19; 20:1, 4, 11; 21:1). The secondary phrase "I also saw" is not in the Greek, but is added for ease in some English translations. Following the culmination of the recompense to the harlot city, Rome (Revelation 17–18), there is a transitional vision (actually a "hearing," see 19:1 and 19:6) that introduces the theme of the marriage feast of the Lamb (19:1–10). The marriage feast theme anticipates the seventh and final vision: the new Jerusalem (21:1ff.), which we will consider in the next chapter.

Typical of what is seen throughout the book of Revelation, these visions are not incremental in an objectifying, logical way. In other words, the visions remain images that are notoriously loose about details that would tie them up in a neat, consistent fashion. Of the final set of visions, we can ask questions like "Over whom do the participants in the thousand-year kingdom reign (20:4), if all the nations are dead (see 19:18, 21)?" Our curious demand for such details is like asking such questions as "How did the serpent talk in the Garden of Eden?" and "Where did Cain find his wife?"

Each vision builds toward the culmination, but not in linear fashion. In some ways it might be compared to our dreams. Dreams are full of visuals, often with no logical consistency. People you know from one part of your life appear in different settings. You leave a room, return, and find the room not the same. Often there is a through-line, a thematic connection, but the visual representations are not entirely consistent.

The First Four Visions

The through-line that ties together these last seven visions of Revelation is marked by the first and last visions. The first vision is the coming of the conquering Christ (19:11–16); the last vision, the eternal kingdom of God in its final and fullest expression (21:1ff.). What stands between these two "bookends" is the final resolution of the powers of evil.

After the first vision of the conquering Christ, riding the white horse, who is "King of kings and Lord of lords" (19:11–16), the second vision is the angelic announcement of a feast, which is

> "Here is no calendarization of the End, but a tour through an eschatological art gallery in which the theme of God's victory at the end of history is treated in seven different pictures, each complete in itself with its own message and with little concern for chronology."
> —Boring, *Revelation*, Interpretation, 195.

an ironic imitation of the great marriage feast. This feast is for vultures and buzzards. Their meal will be the flesh of those who war against the Lamb (19:17–18).

The third vision is the gathering for war against the Lamb (19:19–21). What is intriguing is that in a literary piece such as Revelation, so oriented to graphic detail, there is no description of a battle or war. Just when we expect graphics to make *Star Wars*–style battle scenes pale in comparison, there is no battle! The sea beast and the false prophet (the land beast) are simply thrown into the lake of fire, their human followers are killed and given over to the vultures, and only Satan is left to be dealt with. *In the ultimate sense, there is no contest between good and evil, because the Lamb has already conquered at Golgotha.*

With 20:1–3, we come to the fourth vision. The non-battle has taken care of all the enemies except Satan. Lest we miss this combatant, we are given all four names: dragon, serpent, Devil, and Satan (20:2). Satan is bound by an angel, not by Christ, for a thousand years. Here is where the term "millennium" is derived: from Latin *mille* (thousand) and *annus* (year). The purpose of the binding is specifically declared: "so that he would deceive the nations no more, until the thousand years were ended" (20:3). This vision anticipates Satan's release for "a little while" (20:3).

> "There is no ultimate dualism. The power of evil, deadly real though it be, is temporary and finally operates by permission of the one God."—Boring, *Revelation*, Interpretation, 202.

The Millennial Kingdom

The fifth vision (20:4–10) gives the content of the millennium and the little while that will follow the millennium. The content of the millennium is the "first resurrection" (20:5). What is not completely clear is who participates in this first resurrection. Grammatically, the middle part of 20:4 can be rendered in one of two ways:

> I also saw the souls of those who had been beheaded for their testimony to Jesus and for the word of God. They had not worshiped the beast or its image and had not received its mark on their foreheads or their hands. (NRSV)

> I saw the souls of all who had been beheaded for having witnessed for Jesus and for having preached God's word, and those who refused to

worship the beast or his statue and would not accept the brand—mark on their foreheads or hands. (New Jerusalem Bible)

The difference in these two readings is a question of how many groups are described. The NRSV translation implies that only those who are martyred are part of this "first resurrection." The NJB implies that there are two groups: martyrs and those who were faithful confessors of the faith.

Grammatically, both readings can be argued. In one understanding, if there is only one group, then only those who were martyred for their faith participate in the millennial kingdom. That is to say, if some do not die for their faith, they do not join in the millennial kingdom. However, the understanding of two groups is also plausible because the description of the participants in the millennial kingdom echoes declarations in Revelation made to *all* the faithful, martyrs and confessors alike. The participants in the millennial kingdom are promised that the "second death" will have no power over them (20:6). This same promise was made to all the faithful in Smyrna, "those who conquer" (2:9). Likewise, the description of millennial participants ruling with Christ (20:6) is echoed in the conquering promise to those in Thyatira (2:26) and Laodicea (3:21). Given the context of the letters to the churches, those conquering are all who will not compromise the faith, those who risk martyrdom and those martyred.

In addition, the participants in the millennial kingdom are made "priests" (20:6). This description echoes an earlier declaration: "[Jesus Christ] made us to be a kingdom, priests serving his God and Father" (1:6). This declaration applies to all the faithful, martyrs and confessors.

Given the parallel between the promises made to all the faithful, martyrs and confessors alike, the participants in the millennial kingdom are likely intended to be all the faithful. (See Boring, 204–5, who argues for *one* group, the martyred church which includes *all* the faithful. Boring concedes that though not all the faithful will be martyred, John refers to all the faithful in this manner.) Thus, in this fifth vision, the content of the first resurrection is the inclusion of all the faithful in a thousand-year rule with Christ. Before addressing the "why" of the millennial kingdom, we need to finish out this fifth vision: the "little while" of Satan's release.

Satan is released and sets out on the task of deceiving the nations again. These enemies are "Gog and Magog," a reference to Ezekiel 38–39. Boring notes:

By John's time, Jewish tradition had long since transformed the "Gog of Magog" [see Ezek. 38–39] into "Gog and Magog" and made them into the ultimate enemies of God's people to be destroyed in the eschatological battle. . . . For John, too, evil as embodied in historical individuals and nations is not the ultimate enemy. By "Gog and Magog" we should not think of historical nations that have had a continuing existence during the preceding scene of the millennium, nor of nations of our own time "predicted" by biblical prophecy. John is preparing to present before our imaginations a picture of the ultimate destruction of evil and needs for this scene antagonists to God who are larger than life. (Boring, 209)

 Want to Know More?

About the millennium? See N. T. Wright, *The Millennium Myth: Hope for a Postmodern World* (Louisville, Ky.: Westminster John Knox Press, 1999).

About prophetic and apocalyptic eschatologies? See M. Eugene Boring, *Revelation*, Interpretation, 206–7 and Charles H. Talbert, *The Apocalypse: A Reading of the Revelation of John* (Louisville, Ky.: Westminster John Knox Press, 1994), 91–94.

Filling out this fifth vision of the "little while" of Satan's release, there is another final non-battle (as in 19:17–21 and 11:17–19). Then Satan joins his cohorts, the sea beast and the false prophet, in the lake of fire, the ultimate and final demise.

"Without any struggle, fire comes from heaven and destroys the enemies of God's people, and the devil disappears into the lake of fire forever. This is another affirmation of the apocalyptist's view that, while we must responsibly resist evil, 'deliver us from evil' is a prayer that finally must be answered from God's side."—Boring, *Revelation*, Interpretation, 210.

The Apocalyptic Tradition

The fourth and fifth visions (20:1–10) of the millennial kingdom and Satan's last stand are not easy to understand and have been heaped with various interpretations, often involving "the Rapture." The book of Revelation, indeed the entire New Testament, does not use this word. To find the Rapture in Revelation, you have to come to the text with a preconception in mind; the text itself gives no such indication. Far more fruitful for understanding this text is the literary and theological heritage of apocalyptic literature.

The conception of a millennial kingdom is not original to John. It is part of his heritage, part of his theological vocabulary. Reflections about "end things" or eschatology followed two major strands in the centuries before John: prophetic and apocalyptic. Prophetic eschatology, particularly seen in most of the Old Testament prophets, anticipated a this-worldly fulfillment or culmination of history. For example, the vision of the peaceful kingdom of Isaiah and Micah is the beating of swords into plowshares and spears into pruning hooks, with nations giving up warfare (Isa. 2:2–4; Micah 4:1–5)—a perfection of this world.

Apocalyptic eschatology, in contrast, viewed this world as too broken and ruined by evil to be rescued or restored. The present world must pass away for a new heaven and new earth (see Isa. 65:16; 66:22; 2 Peter 3:12–13). The Messiah is thus an otherworldly, transcendent figure who brings a new kingdom, "not of this world."

These two eschatologies were melded together, giving a three-step culmination of history with the end of this world, a transitional kingdom, and then a transcendent, eternal kingdom.

> By John's time, these two views had already been combined into a scheme in which a this-worldly messiah brought this-worldly salvation during a transitional kingdom, which was then superseded by eternal apocalyptic salvation in the new world. (Boring, 207)

This synthesis of prophetic and apocalyptic eschatologies makes sense of many of the elements in the fourth and fifth visions. We find, for example, other apocalyptic literature with transitional kingdoms of varying lengths of time: 40, 400, 365, 365,000, 7,000, and, like John's number, 1,000 years. In addition, this synthesis between the two eschatologies may make sense of the language about the first resurrection and the second death, particularly if the first resurrection implies a second. In other words, there is the resurrection life of the millennial kingdom and then of the final, eternal kingdom (21:1ff.).

Finally, since both prophetic and apocalyptic eschatologies expect end-time battles, John sees two end-time battles. In the first, the Messiah (and angels, 19:14) fight and win. In the second, God intervenes directly (20:9b).

John's millennial kingdom is part of the apocalyptic tradition that he inherits. In addition, he is also following the basic sequence of Ezekiel 37–48. The first resurrection and millennial kingdom corresponds to the restoration of the dry bones and the rule of David (Ezekiel 37). The defeat of Gog and

---

How many resurrections are there?

References in 20:5 to "the first resurrection" lead some to conclude that there will be another. Some ancient writings refer to stages of resurrection, where earthly bodies will be raised on earth and then transformed later into immortality (see Talbert, *The Apocalypse*, 94). Others defend one resurrection stating that John was combatting opponents who claimed the resurrection had occurred already (see Boring, *Revelation, Interpretation*, 208).

Magog corresponds to a similar account in Ezekiel 37–39. The coming of the Holy City (in the seventh vision, 21:1ff.) corresponds to a similar vision of a new Jerusalem in Ezekiel 40–48. In other words, the sequence of John's visions fits the broad pattern found in Ezekiel.

The Meaning of the Visions

Given the precedent for John's vision, still to be answered is what is the theological purpose of Satan's binding, the millennial kingdom, the release of Satan, the final deception of the nations, and final defeat of Satan. In other words, what is the message of these visions?

The purpose of Satan's binding is explicitly stated: "he would deceive the nations no more" (20:3). While Satan is bound, the world is deception-free. Human beings take their place ruling the earth, fulfilling the calling of Genesis 1:26–29 to have dominion over the earth. The millennial kingdom is human life as we are created to live it. The prophetic eschatology of a this-worldly kingdom is complete.

However, with the release of Satan and the resurrection of the nations ("The rest of the dead did not come to life until the thousand years were ended," 20:5), the issue becomes, what choices will human beings make? The same pattern of choices is followed. Satan takes up the task and the nations follow.

> God goes to great extremes. He binds the deceiver and sets up a period of time in which His will is perfectly clear and obvious to all. The hope is that to do so will elicit the repentance of the nations. Nevertheless, it is all to no avail. When the deceiver is set free, the deceiver still finds the hearts of humans responsive to his seductiveness. (Talbert, 95)

The millennial kingdom is the final effort to elicit repentance, an effort that follows up on the tribulation/judgment begun in history (9:20–21; 19:9, 11, 21): a tribulation that sought the same repentance. To put it in the simplest terms, the tribulation is the stick and the millennial kingdom is the carrot. The expectation of the fourth and fifth visions is that God's extreme measures leave humans without excuse.

In some ways these two visions are like the concluding conversation be-

> "Evil does not die quickly. Even the thousand years of peace have not ended the ease with which some will follow Satan when he makes his appearance."
> —González and González, *Revelation*, Westminster Bible Companion, 133.

tween Dives (the traditional name of the rich man) and Abraham in Jesus' parable in Luke 16:19–31. Dives, in the torment of Hades, asks that someone go and warn his five brothers to repent and avoid Dives' fate. Abraham replies that his brothers have Moses and the prophets to teach them. Dives says that more is needed; someone must rise from the dead and go to them. Abraham replies "If they do not listen to Moses and the prophets, neither will they be convinced even if someone rises from the dead" (Luke 16:31). Even a thousand-year reign of the saints with Christ, proclaims the Seer, does not change the human predilection to follow the great deceiver, Satan.

The sixth vision is fittingly the "final judgment." All the dead are gathered before the throne. Fitting for the transition to a more apocalyptic eschatology, earth and heaven flee from his presence (20:11). Typical of the Seer's perspective on the heavenly throne, the occupant on the throne could be God or Christ: Christ as the representative of God or God as defined through Christ. The roles of judge and savior are not separated.

All the dead, great and small, stand before the throne. The basis of the judgment appears at first to be twofold: what deeds are recorded in the books and what names are recorded in the book of life. The books establish the criteria of judgment: human deeds. However, it is not all dependent on what a person does. The important book, the one that counts, is the book of life. The New Testament tension of grace and works is evident here. What a person does matters. Works are the basis for judgment. However, works are not the final criteria. The book of life is the deciding factor. In pictorial terms, the Seer lays out the paradox of grace and works.

> "At the last judgment, Death and Hades are thrown into the lake of fire. It is the death of Death."—Boring, *Revelation*, Interpretation, 213.

We are ultimately responsible for what we do, for it has eternal consequences—we are judged by works. God is ultimately responsible for our salvation, it is his deed that saves, not ours—we are saved by grace. Propositional language will always sound paradoxical on such ultimate issues; John's pictorial language makes both statements. (Boring, 212)

The visions that fall between the second coming of Christ and the final eternal kingdom are not easy to understand and leave many questions. In particular, the vision of the millennial kingdom is only a small part of the total movement that culminates in the "new heaven and new earth" of Revelation 21. As we have noted all along, there is little concern for strict chronology in Revelation. For example, each series of seven—the seals (6:1–17; 8:1–6), trumpets (8:7–21; 11:15–19), and bowls (16:1–21)—reaches a final and perfect culmination. However, after each of these culminations, there are more visions. In the first series of seven seals, the sixth seal of 6:12–17 describes the dissolution of the world. From a chronological perspective, one wonders what else could be said about history. Yet John still has much to say!

This last set of visions is just one more series and is the only one to include a reference to the millennial kingdom. As we noted at the beginning of this unit, there are themes more central in the book of Revelation than the millennial kingdom. And more central to this final visionary sequence of seven is the salvific vision of chapter 21, to which we now will turn.

Questions for Reflection:

1. This unit discusses the use of images borrowed from a tradition of literature like Revelation. How does this knowledge influence your understanding of scripture? Check the references in Daniel, Ezekiel, etc., cited in this unit. How have these familiar images been incorporated into Revelation? How have they changed?
2. In this chapter are images of books of deeds and a book of life (20:12). What are some other passages in scripture that refer to grace, faith, or works? How does one reconcile the tension between grace and works? Which is more important: good deeds, correct doctrine, faith, or some combination of two or all three? Why or why not?
3. This unit states that the image of "a thousand-year reign of the saints with Christ . . . does not change the human predilection to follow . . . Satan." This is a strong statement. Is this really the case? Why or why not?
4. Knowing you are studying the book of Revelation, if someone were to say to you, "We are living in the last days," how would you respond?

Revelation 21:1–22:5 ▮10

All Things New

John's final vision is fittingly his best and his most developed: the new Jerusalem, the heavenly city. As Boring carefully lays out (214–16), John's vision is not original in the sense of being new material: the elements of his vision are drawn from Jewish traditions and from Hellenistic/Roman aspirations about the ideal city. John's vision is a carefully crafted literary piece and not an ecstatic vision. In other words, John's vision is not an objective documentary of one who has "been there." Once again, we have the artist, drawing from the available colors of his tradition, who gives us a new way to see things.

> "What awaits the believer and the world at the End of all things? John's first and last word is 'God.'"—Boring, *Revelation,* Interpretation, 216.

The new way to see is more than just seeing golden streets and pearly gates: we see God. John's faith heritage was that no mortal can see God. Even Moses, who was on intimate terms with God, was permitted only to see God's "back" (Ex. 33:17–23; see also Ex. 34:29–35). The descent of the heavenly city is the dwelling of God with humanity; God speaks and says "I am the Alpha and the Omega, . . . the beginning and the end" (Rev. 22:13). Boring (215) puts it this way:

> Shining through the varied pictures of "what it will be like" is the conviction which John shares with Paul that at the end of the historical road God will be "all in all" (*panta en pasin,* RSV "everything to everyone," I Cor. 15:28) . . . God does not merely bring the End, God *is* the End.

89

In looking at this entire vision, we will consider three major aspects: the series of "noes" and "nots" in the vision; the energetic tension between present and future; and the characteristics of the heavenly city.

The Via Negativa

Boring (216) has aptly noted that John's vision, though not a philosophical discourse, utilizes the philosophical pattern of the *via negativa,* "the negative way." That is, while we cannot always say what the transcendent world of God is like, we can with more assurance say what it *is not* like. John's vision has a series of "noes" and "nots."

1. *No sea (21:1).* Although we may be the kind of people that find the sea a calming, relaxing setting, it was not so for John and his theological tradition. The sea represents chaotic power that strives against the creative power of God (see Gen. 1:2). At the seashore the dragon takes his stand against the saints, and out of the sea comes the dragon's great minion, the sea beast (12:18; 13:1). And in existential terms, the sea is what stands between John, the pastor, on the island of Patmos and his congregations in Asia. In John's heavenly vision, there is no chaotic power to threaten or separate.

2. *No tears, death, sorrow, crying, pain (21:4).* This comforting "no" rings out in the church's witness to the resurrection at funeral or memorial services. "Here the Almighty himself promises that all that now robs life from being fulfilled, joyful, vibrant *life* will be absent from the transcendent reality to which he is leading history" (Boring, 217).

3. *No cowardly, faithless, polluted, murderers, fornicators, sorcerers, idolaters, or liars (21:8).* John's listing of vices is comparable to other New Testament listings but, as usual, not without some added nuance to fit his pastoral situation. The first and last in the listings—the two places of preeminence—are not general statements; they reflect the lack of courage before Roman courts and the lack of truthfulness in declaring the faith. Likewise, the other terms reflect the sins that are particularly associated with the emperor cult and the pressures of pagan society.

"Nothing evil, nothing unclean, will be able to contaminate or corrupt the new Jerusalem."—González and González, *Revelation,* Westminster Bible Companion, 143.

4. *No temple (21:22).* Here John breaks with a major tradition that has guided his thought, particularly from 19:1 on. Ezekiel 37–48 has been the model for his sequence and for many of the details of his vision. However, Ezekiel 40–48 has a detailed depiction of the temple in the new Jerusalem. John's vision has no temple, no set-apart sacred space where we meet God in a more in-depth way. In other words, there is no place to go to church in the heavenly city. Shirley Guthrie voices one happy opinion about this: "What a relief to know that it will not be like being in church all the time! What could be more boring than to spend eternity sitting around singing hymns, listening to sermons, praying, and listening to prayers (some of which already seem to last forever)!" (p. 389). There will be no need for the church; our mission will be done. God will be all and in all.

5. *No sun, moon, or night (21:23; 22:5).* Like the Genesis creation story, where light is created before sun, moon, or stars, there is light in the heavenly city without need of celestial bodies. God is that glorious light.

> "God's presence in the city at once banishes night and all its anxieties and makes all other forms of light irrelevant."—Boring, *Revelation*, Interpretation, 218.

6. *No closed gates (21:25).* In part because it is always day, there is no need to shut the gates of the city. No closed gates implies more. Entrance into the city is open to all who would enter. Peace and security reign.

7. *No curse (22:3).* The curse of Genesis 3:1–6 is lifted. The heavenly city rings with "Joy to the world. . . . He comes to make his blessings flow far as the curse is found."

The "noes" and "nots" of this heavenly vision are the negative way of declaring a positive of the new Jerusalem.

The Future and Present

Søren Kierkegaard, a Danish theologian of the nineteenth century, once wrote: "Life can only be understood backward, but it must be lived forward." Kierkegaard was saying that one day life will be clear. One day we will say, "Oh, I see." But we live our lives forward. And living life forward means a certain amount of ignorance and not knowing. Living life forward means saying: "The grace of God is still to be seen."

The seer of the book of Revelation, John, with this vision of a new heaven and a new earth, saw the future realm of God. He saw the future. He offers us the opportunity to understand life, not by looking backward from our present, but by looking backward from his vision of a new heaven and new earth. Indeed, the confidence of the Christian hope in reading this passage at funerals, as is frequently done, is the perspective that life will be understood, looking backward and seeing from the perspective of the vision. God's home will be with the faithful and there will be no tears, suffering, or death anymore.

> "The figure on the throne creates the sensation of overwhelming power and authority. We are meant to feel the way Dorothy and her friends felt when they first met the Wizard of Oz."—C. Freeman Sleeper, *The Victorious Christ*, 24.

John's vision in chapter 21, however, is more than a far-off goal, more than a distant possibility, more than a wished-for end of all things. As is generally true of the other visions, the grammar is ambiguously stated in the past or present tense. Is John talking about the future, or is he talking about what is just beyond our senses? Is he talking about something that has not happened, or something that we just have not had the sense to see, hear, smell, taste, or touch?

The vision gives us a clue that even now the heavenly city, the new Jerusalem, is in the process of being realized. For a literal reading of chapter 21 yields an absurd sort of conclusion: the city descends from heaven twice. The opening vision is of the descent of the new Jerusalem: "And I saw the holy city, the new Jerusalem, coming down out of heaven from God, prepared as a bride adorned for her husband" (21:2). Note the grammar of "I saw"—the past tense. It is an accomplished fact within the vision. It has happened. Then, after a word from God about being the beginning and the end, the Alpha and the Omega, John is guided by an angel to a great and high mountain where, says John, the angel "showed me the holy city Jerusalem coming down out of heaven from God" (21:10).

Hold on! Did it come down twice? Did the holy city somehow make a trial approach the first time and then arrive the second time, like an airplane buzzing the tower and coming back to land? A literal reading of the chapter leads to absurd sorts of conclusions.

Or maybe it is that the holy city is always in the state of descending, even in the present time. Maybe this is not just a future event, but something that is happening for John and his readers in the now. Could it not be that John's vision is of what is in process now, just beyond our senses? John cracks the window shades on this room we call reality, and we catch a glimpse of God's world surrounding us, just beyond the walls of reality:

> Heaven is not remote, either in time or space, but immediate. Heaven is not what we wait for until the rapture or where we go when we die, but what is barely out of the range of our senses but brought to our senses by St. John's visions. . . . The vision of heaven is an affirmation of the correspondence: that which we have begun to experience corresponds to what we will completely experience. The vision of heaven is not the promise of anything other than what we have already received by faith; it does, though, promise more, namely, its completion. (Peterson, 172)

Heaven begins on earth. It is the invisible to which we are drawn now, that will develop into full visibility. The features of this heavenly vision correspond to what we already know. The poet Elizabeth Barrett Browning, alluding to Moses taking off his shoes before the burning bush, puts it this way:

> Earth's crammed with heaven,
> And every common bush afire with God;
> But only he who sees takes off his shoes;
> The rest sit round it and pluck blackberries.
>
> (*Aurora Leigh,* VII, 821–24)

Heaven is the affirmation that the good— the good that we experience, that we practice, that we strive for—is already immersed in a deeper, more real reality. The beauties and sacred moments of this life—tree and rock, beach and mountain, baptism and Lord's Supper, the cross and Jesus—these are not illusions that trick us now into what cynics might think of as naive, useless, and silly faith. Earth's crammed with heaven—that is the vision of John—but then comes the surprise.

> "The splendour of God is used to satisfy the thirst of the longing heart."—William Barclay, *The Revelation of John,* vol. 2, Daily Study Bible, 205.

The Heavenly City

The surprise in John's vision is that although Garden of Eden themes are a part of the vision, the dominant theme is that of the heavenly city, the new Jerusalem. In other words, heaven is marked by *city life* and not *garden life*.

The biblical precedent for heaven would seem to be more garden-like. Following the first story of the Bible, humanity was expelled from the garden. Salvation could well be expressed in terms of restoration: a return to Eden. Indeed, Jesus promises the thief on the cross: "Truly I tell you, today you will be with me in Paradise" (Luke 23:43). "Paradise" is used in the Greek Old Testament (LXX) to refer to the Garden of Eden. The root of the word is Persian, meaning "garden" or "forest."

John's heavenly vision has Paradise themes: e.g., the river of life, the tree of life, no curse (22:1–3). However, the dominant theme of his vision is urban. Gardens are ordered by God (Joyce Kilmer's line about "only God can make a tree"); cities are ordered by human beings. Gardens tend to be quiet and apt for individual meditation; cities are busy, loud, and crowded. Boring (219) notes: "A city is the realization of human community, the concrete living out of interdependence as the essential nature of human life."

The biblical track record of cities, however, is not good, to say the least. The first city, Enoch, is built by Cain, the first murderer (Gen. 4:17). The second great city is Babel, built by those who would lift themselves up to God (Gen. 11:1ff.). The names of Sodom and Gomorrah are now proverbial images for the depravity of cities (Gen. 18:16ff.). Jerusalem has a mixed review. At times, it was the "holy city of Zion"; at other times, a city beset by repeated destruction because of the people's faithlessness. Jesus himself would weep over the city of Jerusalem, particularly for its rejection of him. Just decades before the writing of Revelation, Jerusalem was demolished by Roman armies, followed by an edict that would not permit Jews to come back to the Temple Mount, much less to rebuild the Temple. Finally, the city of Rome receives a scathing review in the visions of John (see Rev. 17:1ff.).

To the urban Christians of the seven cities of the province of Asia, John provides a city-shaped vision of heaven:

Want to Know More?

About Moses seeing only the backside of God? See Terence E. Fretheim, *Exodus*, Interpretation (Lousiville, Ky.: John Knox Press, 1991), 299–301.

About significance of Jerusalem to the Jews? See Werner H. Schmidt, *The Faith of the Old Testament: A History* (Philadelphia: Westminster Press, 1983), 207–20.

About the concept of Paradise? See Leland Ryken, James C. Wilhoit, and Tremper Longman III, eds., *Dictionary of Biblical Imagery* (Downers Grove, Ill.: InterVarsity Press, 1998), 315–17.

Heaven is formed out of dirty streets and murderous alleys, adulterous bedrooms and corrupt courts, hypocritical synagogues and commercialized churches, thieving tax-collectors and traitorous disciples: a city, but now a holy city. (Peterson, 174)

There is no escapism here, no release from responsibilities, no long (eternal) weekend away from it all. Heaven is connected to brother-hating (Enoch), God-defying (Babel), loose-living (Sodom and Gomorrah), Christ-rejecting (Jerusalem), and church-persecuting (Rome).

The character of this renewed city is developed in several ways:

1. A particular city, Jerusalem, connected to the heritage of the people of God (a rich repository of images for church music: "Glorious Things of Thee Are Spoken, Zion City of our God," "Jerusalem the Golden, With Milk and Honey Blest," "O Holy City, Seen of John," "The Holy City," and so forth).
2. A renewed city, where the mistakes and misdirections of all prior cities are corrected (God does not make all *new* things but *all things* new—21:5).
3. A big, inclusive city, bringing together peoples and nations (21:3, 26; 22:2—like the best of the melting pot of New York City with its multitude of racial and ethnic residents).
4. A beautiful city that is a delight to the senses: gold, jewels, and pearls ("O What a Beautiful City" is a refrain of an African American spiritual).
5. A holy city where, as Boring (222–23) notes, people do more than pious acts but are oriented to God's will.
6. An active city where people do not rest in peace but are engaged in worthwhile and fulfilling activity. (The Seer does not satisfy our curiosity about what we "will do" beyond worshiping and reigning.)

"Mourning and crying and pain will be no more" (21:4). View of the Wailing Wall in Jerusalem

Each of these characteristics warrants further development; I will develop only the last one. John's vision of an active city continues to connect identity and vocation, being and doing. Heaven is not eternal nothingness. We continue to have work to do.

Rudyard Kipling, using the theme of oil painting, wrote a poem that captures this conception.

> When Earth's last picture is painted, and the tubes are twisted and dried,
> When the oldest colours have faded, and the youngest critic has died,
> We shall rest, and, faith, we shall need it—lie down for an aeon or two,
> Till the Master of All Good Workmen shall put us to work anew.
>
> And those that were good shall be happy; they shall sit in a golden chair;
> They shall splash at a ten-league canvas with brushes of comets' hair.
> They shall find real saints to draw from—Magdalene, Peter, and Paul;
> They shall work for an age at a sitting, and never be tired at all!
>
> And only The Master shall praise us, and only The Master shall blame;
> And no one shall work for money, and no one shall work for fame;
> But each for the joy of the working, and each, in his separate star,
> Shall draw the Thing as he sees It for the God of Things as They Are!

("L'Envoi")

Kipling's poem, though perhaps overly individualistic, captures the Seer's theme of activity in the heavenly city.

John the Seer saves his best sight for last. The wrapper is torn away from the present, and our vision is finally clear. Beneath lies a gift too beautiful to believe, yet it is what our heart always longed for—sparkling, tear-repelling, pain-erasing, everlasting light. For people numbed by the ordinary, dazed by the pressures, and blinded by the suffering, he proclaims the good news, that "the Lord God will be their light, and they will reign forever and ever" (22:5).

? Questions for Reflection

1. Revelation 22:1 mentions "the river of the water of life." In John 4:7–14, Jesus uses a similar image in his discussion with the woman of Samaria. What do you think is being referred to here? Revelation 22:2 mentions "the healing of the nations." What do you think that means? How are the nations in need of healing?
2. This unit suggests that some of Heaven may be glimpsed now. What are some examples of glimpses of heaven of which you are aware?
3. Revelation begins with letters to cities and ends with a description of a new city. What are some other examples of repetition or re-

casting of images in Revelation? What are some examples of the contrast of images with their opposites?

4. In your opinion, what are the dominant themes of the book of Revelation? Would you characterize its message as "good news" or "bad news?" Why? Do you agree or disagree with John's vision? Why?

Bibliography

Barclay, William. *The Revelation of John.* 2 vols. Rev. ed. Daily Study Bible. Philadelphia: Westminster Press, 1976.

Boring, M. Eugene. Revelation. *Interpretation.* Louisville, Ky.: John Knox Press, 1989.

Charlesworth, James H., ed. *The Old Testament Pseudepigrapha.* 2 vols. Garden City, N.Y.: Doubleday & Co., 1983–85.

Chesterton, G. K. *Orthodoxy.* New York: John Lane Co., 1908.

Collins, Adela Yarbro. "Reading the Book of Revelation in the Twentieth Century." *Interpretation* 40, no. 3 (July 1986): 229–42.

Eichrodt, Walther. *Theology of the Old Testament.* Vol. 1. Philadelphia: Westminster Press, 1961.

González, Catherine Gunsalus, and Justo L. González. *Revelation.* Westminster Bible Companion. Louisville, Ky.: Westminster John Knox Press, 1997.

Guthrie, Shirley C. *Christian Doctrine.* Rev. ed. Louisville, Ky.: Westminster John Knox Press, 1994.

Kelly, Balmer H. "Revelation 7:9–17." *Interpretation* 40, no. 3 (July 1986): 288–95.

King, Martin Luther, Jr. *Strength to Love.* In *A Martin Luther King Treasury.* Yonkers, N.Y.: Educational Heritage, 1964.

Mounce, Robert H. *The Book of Revelation.* Grand Rapids: Wm. B. Eerdmans Publishing Co., 1977.

Peterson, Eugene. *Reversed Thunder: The Revelation of John and the Praying Imagination.* San Francisco: Harper & Row, 1988.

Sleeper, C. Freeman. *The Victorious Christ: A Study of the Book of Revelation.* Louisville, Ky.: Westminster John Knox Press, 1996.

Talbert, Charles H. *The Apocalypse: A Reading of the Revelation of John.* Louisville, Ky.: Westminster John Knox Press, 1996.

Interpretation Bible Studies
Leader's Guide

Interpretation Bible Studies (IBS), for adults and older youth, are flexible, attractive, easy-to-use, and filled with solid information about the Bible. IBS helps Christians discover the guidance and power of the scriptures for living today. Perhaps you are leading a church school class, a midweek Bible study group, or a youth group meeting, or simply using this in your own personal study. Whatever the setting may be, we hope you find this *Leader's Guide* helpful. Since every context and group is different, this *Leader's Guide* does not presume to tell you how to structure Bible study for your situation. Instead, the *Leader's Guide* seeks to offer choices—a number of helpful suggestions for leading a successful Bible study using IBS.

> "The church that no longer hears the essential message of the Scriptures soon ceases to understand what it is for and is open to be captured by the dominant religious philosophy of the moment." —James D. Smart, *The Strange Silence of the Bible in the Church: A Study in Hermeneutics* (Philadelphia: Westminster Press, 1970), 10.

How Should I Teach IBS?

1. Explore the Format

There is a wealth of information in IBS, perhaps more than you can use in one session. In this case, more is better. IBS has been designed to give you a well-stocked buffet of content and teachable insights. Pick and choose what suits your group's needs. Perhaps you will want to split units into two or more sessions, or combine units into a single session. Perhaps you will decide to use only a portion of a unit and then move on to the next unit. *There is not a structured theme or teaching focus to each unit that must be followed for IBS to be used.* Rather, IBS offers the flexibility to adjust to whatever suits your context.

> "The more we bring to the Bible, the more we get from the Bible." —William Barclay, *A Beginner's Guide to the New Testament* (Louisville, Ky.: Westminster John Knox Press, 1995), vii.

A recent survey of both professional and volunteer church educators revealed that their number-one concern was that Bible study materials be teacher-friendly. IBS is indeed teacher-friendly in two important ways. First, since IBS provides abundant content and a flexible design, teachers can shape the lessons creatively, responding to the needs of the group and employing a wide variety of teaching methods. Second, those who wish more specific suggestions for planning the sessions can find them at the Westminster John Knox Press Web site (**www.wjkbooks.com**). Here, you can access a study guide with teaching suggestions for each IBS unit as well as helpful quotations, selections from Bible dictionaries and encyclopedias, and other teaching helps.

IBS is not only teacher-friendly, it is also discussion-friendly. Given the opportunity, most adults and young people relish the chance to talk about the kind of issues raised in IBS. The secret, then, is to determine what works with your group, what will get them to talk. Several good methods for stimulating discussion are presented in this *Leader's Guide,* and once you learn your group, you can apply one of these methods and get the group discussing the Bible and its relevance in their lives.

The format of every IBS unit consists of several features:

a. Body of the Unit. This is the main content, consisting of interesting and informative commentary on the passage and scholarly insight into the biblical text and its significance for Christians today.

b. Sidebars. These are boxes that appear scattered throughout the body of the unit, with maps, photos, quotations, and intriguing ideas. Some sidebars can be identified quickly by a symbol, or icon, that helps the reader know what type of information can be found in that sidebar. There are icons for illustrations, key terms, pertinent quotes, and more.

c. Want to Know More? Each unit includes a "Want to Know More?" section that guides learners who wish to dig deeper and consult other resources. If your church library does not have the resources mentioned, you can look up the information in other standard Bible dictionaries, encyclopedias, and handbooks, or you can find much of this information at the Geneva Press Web site (see last page of this Guide).

d. Questions for Reflection. The unit ends with questions to help the learners think more deeply about the biblical passage and its pertinence for today. These questions are provided as examples only, and teachers are encouraged both to develop their own list of questions and to gather questions from the group. These discussion questions do not usually have specific "correct" answers. Again, the flexibility of IBS allows you to use these questions at the end of the group time, at the beginning, interspersed throughout, or not at all.

> "The trick is to make the Bible our book." — Duncan S. Ferguson, *Bible Basics: Mastering the Content of the Bible* (Louisville, Ky.: Westminster John Knox Press, 1995), 3.

2. Select a Teaching Method

Here are ten suggestions. The format of IBS allows you to choose what direction you will take as you plan to teach. Only you will know how your lesson should best be designed for your group. Some adult groups prefer the lecture method, while others prefer a high level of free-ranging discussion. Many youth groups like interaction, activity, the use of music, and the chance to talk about their own experiences and feelings. Here is a list of a few possible approaches. Let your own creativity add to the list!

a. Let's Talk about What We've Learned. In this approach, all group members are requested to read the scripture passage and the IBS unit before the group meets. Ask the group members to make notes about the main issues, concerns, and questions they see in the passage. When the group meets, these notes are collected, shared, and discussed. This method depends, of course, on the group's willingness to do some "homework."

b. What Do We Want and Need to Know? This approach begins by having the whole group read the scripture passage together. Then, drawing from your study of the IBS, you, as the teacher, write on a board or flip chart two lists:

(1) Things we should know to better understand this passage (content information related to the passage, for example, historical insights about political contexts, geographical landmarks, economic nuances, etc.), and

> "Although small groups can meet for many purposes and draw upon many different resources, the one resource which has shaped the life of the Church more than any other throughout its long history has been the Bible." —Roberta Hestenes, *Using the Bible in Groups* (Philadelphia: Westminster Press, 1983), 14.

(2) Four or five "important issues we should talk about regarding this passage" (with implications for today—how the issues in the biblical context continue into today, for example, issues of idolatry or fear).

Allow the group to add to either list, if they wish, and use the lists to lead into a time of learning, reflection, and discussion. This approach is suitable for those settings where there is little or no advanced preparation by the students.

c. Hunting and Gathering. Start the unit by having the group read the scripture passage together. Then divide the group into smaller clusters (perhaps having as few as one person), each with a different assignment. Some clusters can discuss one or more of the "Questions for Reflection." Others can look up key terms or people in a Bible dictionary or track down other biblical references found in the body of the unit. After the small clusters have had time to complete their tasks, gather the entire group again and lead them through the study material, allowing each cluster to contribute what it learned.

d. From Question Mark to Exclamation Point. This approach begins with contemporary questions and then moves to the biblical content as a response to those questions. One way to do this is for you to ask the group, at the beginning of the class, a rephrased version of one or more of the "Questions for Reflection" at the end of the study unit. For example, one of the questions at the end of the unit on Exodus 3:1–4:17 in the IBS *Exodus* volume reads,

> Moses raised four protests, or objections, to God's call. Contemporary people also raise objections to God's call. In what ways are these similar to Moses' protests? In what ways are they different?

This question assumes familiarity with the biblical passage about Moses, so the question would not work well before the group has explored the passage. However, try rephrasing this question as an opening exercise; for example:

Here is a thought experiment: Let's assume that God, who called people in the Bible to do daring and risky things, still calls people today to tasks of faith and courage. In the Bible, God called Moses from a burning bush and called Isaiah in a moment of ecstatic worship in the Temple. How do you think God's call is experienced by people today? Where do you see evidence of people saying "yes" to God's call? When people say "no" or raise an objection to God's call, what reasons do they give (to themselves, to God)?

Posing this or a similar question at the beginning will generate discussion and raise important issues, and then it can lead the group into an exploration of the biblical passage as a resource for thinking even more deeply about these questions.

e. Let's Go to the Library. From your church library, your pastor's library, or other sources, gather several good commentaries on the book of the Bible you are studying. Among the trustworthy commentaries are those in the Interpretation series (John Knox Press) and the Westminster Bible Companion series (Westminster John Knox Press). Divide your group into smaller clusters and give one commentary to each cluster (one or more of the clusters can be given the IBS volume instead of a full-length commentary). Ask each cluster to read the biblical passage you are studying and then to read the section of the commentary that covers that passage (if your group is large, you may want to make photocopies of the commentary material with proper permission, of course). The task of each cluster is to name the two or three most important insights they discover about the biblical passage by reading and talking together about the commentary material. When you reassemble the larger group to share these insights, your group will gain not only a variety of insights about the passage but also a sense that differing views of the same text are par for the course in biblical interpretation.

f. Working Creatively Together. Begin with a creative group task, tied to the main thrust of the study. For example, if the study is on the Ten Commandments, a parable, or a psalm, have the group rewrite the Ten Commandments, the parable, or the psalm in contemporary language. If the passage is an epistle, have the group write a letter to their own congregation. Or if the study is a narrative, have the group role-play the characters in the story or write a page describing the story from the point of view of one of the characters. After completion of the task, read and discuss the biblical passage, asking for interpretations and applications from the group and tying in IBS material as it fits the flow of the discussion.

g. Singing Our Faith. Begin the session by singing (or reading) together a hymn that alludes to the biblical passage being studied (or to the theological themes in the passage). Most hymnals have an index of scriptural allusions. For example, if you are studying the unit from the IBS volume on Psalm 121, you can sing "I to the Hills Will Lift My Eyes," "Sing Praise to God, Who Reigns Above," or another hymn based on Psalm 121. Let the group reflect on the thoughts and feelings evoked by the hymn, then move to the biblical passage, allowing the biblical text and the IBS material to underscore, clarify, refine, and deepen the discussion stimulated by the hymn. If you are ambitious, you may ask the group to write a new hymn at the end of the study! (Many hymnals have indexes in the back or companion volumes that help the user match hymns to scripture passages or topics.)

h. Fill in the Blanks. In order to help the learners focus on the content of the biblical passage, at the beginning of the session ask each member of the group to read the biblical passage and fill out a brief questionnaire about the details of the passage (provide a copy for each learner or write the questions on the board). For example, if you are studying the unit in the IBS *Matthew* volume on Matthew 22:1–14, the questionnaire could include questions such as the following:

— In this story, Jesus compares the kingdom of heaven to what?
— List the various responses of those who were invited to the king's banquet but who did not come.
— When his invitation was rejected, how did the king feel? What did the king do?
— In the second part of the story, when the king saw a man at the banquet without a wedding garment, what did the king say? What did the man say? What did the king do?
— What is the saying found at the end of this story?

Gather the group's responses to the questions and perhaps encourage discussion. Then lead the group through the IBS material helping the learners to understand the meanings of these details and the significance of the passage for today. Feeling creative? Instead of a fill-in-the blanks questionnaire, create a crossword puzzle from names and words in the biblical passage.

i. Get the Picture. In this approach, stimulate group discussion by incorporating a painting, photograph, or other visual object into the lesson. You can begin by having the group examine and comment on this visual or you can introduce the visual later in the lesson—it depends on the object used. If, for example, you are studying the unit Exodus 3:1–4:17 in the IBS *Exodus* volume, you may want to view Paul Koli's very colorful painting *The Burning Bush.* Two sources for this painting are *The Bible Through Asian Eyes,* edited by Masao Takenaka and Ron O'Grady (National City, Calif.: Pace Publishing Co., 1991), and *Imaging the Word: An Arts and Lectionary Resource,* vol. 3, edited by Susan A. Blain (Cleveland: United Church Press, 1996).

j. Now Hear This. Especially if your class is large, you may want to use the lecture method. As the teacher, you prepare a presentation on the biblical passage, using as many resources as you have available plus your own experience, but following the content of the IBS unit as a guide. You can make the lecture even more lively by asking the learners at various points along the way to refer to the visuals and quotes found in the "sidebars." A place can be made for questions (like the ones at the end of the unit)—either at the close of the lecture or at strategic points along the way.

> "It is . . . important to call a Bible study group back to what the text being discussed actually says, especially when an individual has gotten off on some tangent." —Richard Robert Osmer, *Teaching for Faith: A Guide for Teachers of Adult Classes* (Louisville, Ky.: Westminster John Knox Press, 1992), 71.

3. Keep These Teaching Tips in Mind

There are no surefire guarantees for a teaching success. However, the following suggestions can increase the chances for a successful study:

a. Always Know Where the Group Is Headed. Take ample time beforehand to prepare the material. Know the main points of the study, and know the destination. Be flexible, and encourage discussion, but don't lose sight of where you are headed.

b. Ask Good Questions; Don't Be Afraid of Silence. Ideally, a discussion blossoms spontaneously from the reading of the scripture. But more often than not, a discussion must be drawn from the group members by a series of well-chosen questions. After asking each question, give the group members time to answer. Let them think, and don't be threatened by a season of silence. Don't feel that every question must have an answer, and that as leader, you must supply every answer. Facilitate discussion by getting the group members to cooperate with each other. Sometimes, the original question can be restated. Sometimes it is helpful to ask a follow-up question like "What makes this a hard question to answer?"

Ask questions that encourage explanatory answers. Try to avoid questions that can be answered simply "Yes" or "No." Rather than asking, "Do you think Moses was frightened by the burning bush?" ask, "What do you think Moses was feeling and experiencing as he stood before the burning bush?" If group members answer with just one word, ask a follow-up question like "Why do you think this is so?" Ask questions about their feelings and opinions, mixed within questions about facts or details. Repeat their responses or restate their response to reinforce their contributions to the group.

> "Studies of learning reveal that while people remember approximately 10% of what they hear, they remember up to 90% of what they say. Therefore, to increase the amount of learning that occurs, increase the amount of talking about the Bible which each member does."—Roberta Hestenes, *Using the Bible in Groups* (Philadelphia: Westminster Press, 1983), 17.

Most studies can generate discussion by asking open-ended questions. Depending on the group, several types of questions can work. Some groups will respond well to content questions that can be answered from reading the IBS comments or the biblical passage. Others will respond well to questions about feelings or thoughts. Still others will respond to questions that challenge them to new thoughts or that may not have exact answers. Be sensitive to the group's dynamic in choosing questions.

Some suggested questions are: What is the point of the passage? Who are the main characters? Where is the tension in the story? Why does it say (this)_____, and not (that) _____? What raises questions for you? What terms need defining? What are the new ideas? What doesn't make sense? What bothers or troubles you about this passage? What keeps you from living the truth of this passage?

c. Don't Settle for the Ordinary. There is nothing like a surprise. Think of special or unique ways to present the ideas of the study. Upset the applecart of the ordinary. Even though the passage may be familiar, look for ways to introduce suspense. Remember that a little mystery can capture the imagination. Change your routine.

Along with the element of surprise, humor can open up a discussion. Don't be afraid to laugh. A well-chosen joke or cartoon may present the central theme in a way that a lecture would have stymied.

Sometimes a passage is too familiar. No one speaks up because everyone feels that all that could be said has been said. Choose an unfamiliar translation from which to read, or if the passage is from a Gospel, compare the story across two or more Gospels and note differences. It is amazing what insights can be drawn from seeing something strange in what was thought to be familiar.

d. Feel Free to Supplement the IBS Resources with Other Material. Consult other commentaries or resources. Tie in current events with the lesson. Scour newspapers or magazines for stories that touch on the issues of the study. Sometimes the lyrics of a song, or a section of prose from a well-written novel, will be just the right seasoning for the study.

e. And Don't Forget to Check the Web. You can download a free study guide from our Web site (**www.wjkbooks.com**). Each study guide includes several possibilities for applying the teaching methods suggested above for individual IBS units.

f. Stay Close to the Biblical Text. Don't forget that the goal is to learn the Bible. Return to the text again and again. Avoid making the mistake of reading the passage only at the beginning of the study, and then wandering away to comments on top of comments from that point on. Trust in the power and presence of the Holy Spirit to use the truths of the passage to work within the lives of the study participants.

> "The Bible is literature, but it is much more than literature. It is the holy book of Jews and Christians, who find there a manifestation of God's presence." —Kathleen Norris, *The Psalms* (New York: Riverhead Books, 1997), xxii.

What If Am Using IBS in Personal Bible Study?

If you are using IBS in your personal Bible study, you can experiment and explore a variety of ways. You may choose to read straight through the study without giving any attention to the sidebars or other features. Or you may find yourself interested in a question or unfamiliar with a key term, and you can allow the sidebars "Want to

Know More?" and "Questions for Reflection" to lead you into deeper learning on these issues. Perhaps you will want to have a few commentaries or a Bible dictionary available to pursue what interests you. As was suggested in one of the teaching methods above, you may want to begin with the questions at the end, and then read the Bible passage followed by the IBS material. Trust the IBS resources to provide good and helpful information, and then follow your interests!

 Want to Know More?

About leading Bible study groups? See Roberta Hestenes, *Using the Bible in Groups* (Philadelphia: Westminster Press, 1983).

About basic Bible content? See Duncan S. Ferguson, *Bible Basics: Mastering the Content of the Bible* (Louisville, Ky.: Westminster John Knox Press, 1995); William M. Ramsay, *The Westminster Guide to the Books of the Bible* (Louisville, Ky.: Westminster John Knox Press, 1994).

About the development of the Bible? See John Barton, *How the Bible Came to Be* (Louisville, Ky.: Westminster John Knox Press, 1997).

About the meaning of difficult terms ? See Donald K. McKim, *Westminster Dictionary of Theological Terms* (Louisville, Ky.: Westminster John Knox Press, 1996); Paul J. Achtemeier, *Harper's Bible Dictionary* (San Francisco: Harper & Row, 1985).

To download a free IBS study guide,

visit our Web site at

www.wjkbooks.com